PUTTING MAN

ON

TRIAL:

Proofs for the Existence of God

LORA ZIEBRO

ISBN 13: 978-0-578-95726-5

CONTENTS

Acknowledgements   7

Part 1: The Courtroom   8

Who is God?   9

Our History: Where It All Began   23

The Character of God   33

The Character of Man   41

Fallen Virtue   47

Is It Relative?   55

GOOD   63

Evil   79

The Law of Love   93

Part 2: The Verdict   100

Who's on Trial?   101

Let's Talk About Justice   111

Jesus: Savior and King   127

Redemption: 139

Why Are We Here? Two Paths   151

The Wrap Up   159

Part 3: Additional Evidence   166

Pain and Suffering: A Testimony of God's Wisdom   167

The God We Are Not   175

Evidence of Artistry and Craftsmanship   183

Something from Someone   199

What is Truth?   205

The God We Need   215

DEDICATION

Dedicated first to Jesus.

Then to: The Wanderer, the Skeptic, the Confused, the Weary and the Faithful.

Lastly, this book is dedicated to my dad. I love you more than words can say.

"Come now, and let us reason together, Says the Lord, Though your sins are like scarlet, They shall be as white as snow; Though they are red like crimson, They shall be as wool."[1]

---

1   Isaiah 1:18 (NKJV)

Acknowledgements

To my Tom...my greatest earthly love and friend. So many roads that I've had the courage to walk through have been because of your encouragement and support! Only Jesus has loved me more. I am forever yours! To my children...There is no better pursuit than Jesus. May you follow Him wildly and fiercely all the days of your life! He is worth it! To Jeff (Mr. Gaines)...You are a true friend...faithful and genuine in all ways. I am blessed by your friendship, help, and wisdom! Thank you for being there through this journey. To my sister Joy, my cousin Dave, my mom and Peggs...Thank you for always being ready to stand by my side, against any storm. To Nate and Sheila Steuer...Thank you for taking time out of your busy schedule to help me along the way. May the Lord continue to bless you and the works of your hands. We are thankful for your friendship and faithful prayers. Soli Deo Gloria! To Pamela Fahs...Thank you for helping me clean up this book and for your faithfulness to its completion. To my students...everyone of you has blessed me and I am thankful for you all. May the Lord use you mightily all the days of your life. He is the greatest adventure!

"Two are better than one because they have a good return for their labor. For if either of them falls, the one will lift up his companion."[2]

2   Ecclesiastes 4:9-10 (NASB)

PART 1:

THE COURTROOM

Who is God?

"If your god is omnipotent, omniscient and omnipresent, then he is a sadist."

Anonymous

"If God is good, why does He allow evil and suffering?" This world seems torn apart and at odds with what many of us have been told about God: that is, He is powerful and good. How can we reconcile a good God and the present existence of evil that we see around us?

When people ask this question, they are essentially calling into question the character of God. The question is less about the evil that occurs and more about the God who allows it. In many ways, at that moment, they are not asking why God has allowed evil and suffering, but rather what type of God would allow it to continue. What they are implying is, "How could You? How dare You? Why would You allow this to happen?" Those individuals are standing in judgement of God, and their question is more of an accusation.

If we are going to put God on trial, then we must consider His defense. I am not saying that God needs a defense or that He has felt the need to defend Himself to us; rather, there is an explanation available if we really want to know why the world is the way that it is.

To answer this question or any other question pertaining to God in relation to us, we must consider the history of mankind and how it relates to our present circumstances. They are incredibly interconnected. Additionally, we must consider the character of God and how His history also pertains to our questions. They too are incredibly interwoven, but for different reasons than the first.

WHAT DO YOU MEAN BY THE WORD "GOD"?

Because the Word of God is the primary tool used to determine these conclusions, before we can begin to delve into why God allows evil to exist, we must first ask a question of greater importance: "What do you mean by the word *God*?" This question is of far greater significance than any other in the area of theology. What we believe about God is the biggest influence on our life. It defines and shapes all that we do, say, and think. If we have a low view of God, we will find ourselves easily judging Him and we'll most likely be doubtful and cynical of the claims of His existence and works on the earth. Conversely, having a proper view of God will help to ground us when life does not make sense. Webster's dictionary defines God in the following way:

"God: the supreme or ultimate reality...such as...the Being perfect in power, wisdom, and goodness who is worshipped as creator and ruler of the universe."[3]

Roughly 55% of the total, global, religious landscape belongs to a religious group with this classic understanding of God.[4] This does not include the religious unaffiliated who also believe in God or a universal Spirit (30% of the religious affiliated in America).[5] While these numbers indicate that the majority of global humankind believe in the classic understanding of God, that does not mean that their view of God is altogether correct. If their God is similar in character to man,

---

3   https://www.merriam-webster.com/dictionary/god Accessed 17 November 2017

4   http://www.pewforum.org/2012/12/18/global-religious-landscape-exec/ Accessed 8 August 2018

5   http://www.pewforum.org/2012/10/09/nones-on-the-rise/ Accessed 8 August 2018

11

inconsistent or changing, apathetic to sin, limited in abilities, or if their view is imbalanced and highlights one attribute of God (love), while dismissing another (holy), their view is inconsistent with the classic definition of God.

THERE ARE SO MANY RELIGIONS OUT THERE...

People have said to me, "There are so many religions out there that it is impossible to know which one is correct." While I do recognize that there are a multitude of religions that are practiced in our world, it *is* possible to know which one is true. If you took a picture of your mother and threw it in a pile that contained hundreds of photos of women, I could easily and reasonably narrow down who she was by eliminating everyone who did not match your description of her. The remaining photos would require closer observation. I would have to look at the clues, facts, evidence, and anything else related to your life to pick her out. Although it would be harder and require greater effort on my part to identify her based on those inferences, it could be done. What I could know for certain was that she was indeed in the pile. No matter how difficult it may be to pinpoint her, finding her would in fact be possible. In the same way, there are clues, facts, and evidence that point to who God is. This process does not eliminate the place for faith. Knowledge in and of itself will not save you, but it will help point you to the One who can.

First, a person has to answer a few questions within themselves before they begin searching for God. This place of self-reflection is where everyone must begin. We have to recognize our already

12

established views of God before we can fully discover who God really is. Ask yourself:

1. Are you willing to accept being wrong about God?

2. Are you willing to consider reasonable arguments even if it challenges your belief?

3. Have you already decided what you are willing to believe?

4. Have you already canceled out any possibilities before you began (i.e., already decided who cannot be God)?

5. Are you willing to accept who God is even if it differs from what you agree with morally?

6. What God are you trying to find - God as He really is or your idea of who God is?

7. Are you willing to let go of the God you have made in your own mind to embrace the God who truly is?

If those questions show an unwillingness to seek out God beyond a preconceived and accepted image, the problem is not lack of evidence for God but rather a lack of willingness to really know Him.

DISQUALIFIED

Any religion whose god is limited, is not the final authority, or is subject to man is naturally disqualified. Their limited position automatically invalidates them from claiming to be God in the classic sense. This is true of any religion in which man:

1. Is his/her own god.

2. Is part of a god.

3. Can become god.

4. Is a god but is unaware of it.

5. Is any variation of these thoughts.

Polytheism would also be disqualified. By its very nature, it worships gods that do not possess the characteristics of God. Multiple, separate beings cannot *each* possess absolute power, knowledge, authority, etc. It is logically impossible for more than one being to possess anything absolutely. Therefore, these gods would be disqualified.

In terms of the view that God is just an impersonal force or non-relational being, we have to contend with the fact of humanity's own personal nature and how we are designed to have relationships. An impersonal force would have no ability to create a personal being as it would have no knowledge, understanding, or conscious awareness to do so. For the same reasons, we could not become personal if our first cause was impersonal. The minute we give it the ability to have that awareness, we can no longer call it an impersonal force. Furthermore, the fact that we are personal, relational beings disqualifies any god or "divine group consciousness" that does not possess the qualities of individual personhood. If we argue that the group consciousness is personal, then the "personal group consciousness" is still limited, because it is shared by multiple essences. Additionally, it would not allow for individuality, because each essence would have a shared nature, a shared morality, and a shared self. Because we are individual

14

by nature, an impersonal force, non-relational being, or divine group consciousness is disqualified by the classic definition of God and is inconsistent with known reality.

Also disqualified would be the belief that God does not exist, because the personal aspect of our nature had to come from somewhere. Science cannot speak about evolution and attribute intelligence, thought, design, and purpose to it; evolution by its very nature does not allow for those possibilities. Those qualities exist among sentient beings not by random chance. Evolution really is at odds with the known world. I will discuss this in greater detail later.

Lastly, any god whose teachings, moral standards, goodness, and character are inconsistent with holiness would be disqualified. Any god who by nature, activity, or command is a promoter of deception, perversion, or immorality is naturally discredited. When considering all other religions and gods, the true God is distinct by His highest example of universal holiness and morality. There is no moral equal to God. By necessity, His nature is the highest in purity. This is not defined by human qualifications of righteousness and good, but by a measure of excellence that is set apart, distinct, and unchanging- in essence, a true north compass of holiness.

WHY IT MATTERS

When dealing with our soul and eternity, we should not entrust it to "a god" but to "The God." We should not be willing to entrust our soul to anyone or anything that does not possess the power to set this universe in motion and keep our soul in eternity. Anyone short of the ultimate authority over all life has no power to grant us more than the temporal world. After all, they cannot grant what they do not possess. We should be looking for absolute truth and unquestionable assurance, both of which are knowable and attainable with God. To get us closer to that point, I believe we can further narrow down the possibilities by examining the clues that surround us.

"THE I AM"

As a Christian, I believe the God of the Bible is the God of all creation and life. I believe the Christian worldview has the best and most thorough explanation of the world as we know it. It has answers to the questions that all people seek to know: who we are, why we are here, who is God, what is wrong with us, etc. It offers a complete history of our universe. Moreover, it is unique among religions in that its overarching message—faith alone—is contrary to the global religious message of faith plus works.

When comparing the God of the Bible to "gods" found in other religions, the God of the Bible best fits the traditional view of "God" for several reasons.

The Judeo-Christian God

1. Claims that He has no one that He is subject to (Revelation 1:8) and that He shares His power/glory with no one (Psalm 62:11, Isaiah 42:8, 48:11). This is ultimately the idea that most of us think of when we use the word "God." We believe that "God" is all powerful: complete, full and total in power.

2. Claims that He is all good (Psalm 136:1).

   *These two primary beliefs, that He is all powerful and that He is all good, are essentially what we call into question when we are thinking about God in relation to the question of evil and suffering.

3. Is monotheistic and, therefore, the top and final authority (Isaiah 43:10).

4. Claims that He is the only true God (Isaiah 43:10).

5. Possesses the attributes that characterize God. He is all powerful (omnipotent)/all good, all knowing (omniscient), always present (omnipresent), eternal, infinite, perfect, unchangeable (immutable), sovereign, holy, faithful, wise, just, self-existent, merciful and loving (He is love).

Additionally, the Bible says that God is the following:

God is God

And God said to Moses, "I AM WHO I AM." And He said, "Thus you shall say to the children of Israel, I AM has sent me to you."[6]

*This verse in Hebrew means "I be that I be." This name speaks to the fact that God is pure existence or what some call "pure actuality." Pure actuality is that which *is* with no possibility not to exist. Put another way, many things can have existence (e.g., human beings, animals, plants), but only one thing can *be* existence. Other things

---

6   Exodus 3:14 (NKJV)

PUTTING MAN ON TRIAL: PROOFS FOR THE EXISTENCE OF GOD

have "being," but only God is "Being."[7]

"Therefore know that the Lord your God, He is God, the faithful God who keeps covenant and mercy for a thousand generations with those who love Him and keep His commandments"[8]

"That they may know that You, whose name alone is the Lord, Are the Most High over all the earth."[9]

God is All Powerful

*"Also God said to him: "I am God **Almighty**...."*[10]

*"Now when Abram was ninety-nine years old, the Lord appeared to Abram and said to him, "I am God **Almighty**; Walk before Me, and be blameless."*[11]

"For since the creation of the world His invisible attributes are clearly seen, being understood by the things that are made, even His eternal power and Godhead, so that they are without excuse."[12]

God is Good

"Oh, give thanks to the Lord, for He is good for His mercy endures forever."[13]

---

7 http://www.gotquestions.org/amp/what-is-God.html Accessed 20 October 2018
8 Deuteronomy 7:9 (NKJV)
9 Psalm 83:18 (NKJV)
10 Genesis 35:11 (NKJV)
11 Genesis 17:1 (NASB)
12 Romans 1:20 (NKJV)
13 Psalm 136:1 (NKJV)

"You are good, and do good; Teach me Your statutes."[14]

"Teach me to do Your will, For You are my God; Your Spirit is good. Lead me in the land of uprightness."[15]

God is Holy

*"And one cried to another and said: 'Holy, **holy**, **holy** is the Lord of hosts; The whole earth is full of His glory!'"*[16]

"...because it is written, 'Be holy, for I am holy.'"[17]

God is All Knowing (Omniscient)

"The eyes of the Lord are in every place, Keeping watch on the evil and the good."[18]

"He counts the number of the stars; He calls them all by name. Great is our Lord, and mighty in power; His understanding is infinite."[19]

God is Sovereign

"I know that You can do everything, And that no purpose of Yours can be withheld from You."[20]

"Whatever the Lord pleases He does, In heaven and in earth, In the seas and in all deep places."[21]

14   Psalm 119:68 (NKJV)
15   Psalm 143:10 (NKJV)
16   Isaiah 6:3 (NKJV)
17   1 Peter 1:16 (NKJV)
18   Proverbs 15:3 (NKJV)
19   Psalm 147:4-5 (NKJV)
20   Job 42:2 (NKJV)
21   Psalm 135:6 (NKJV)

"Declaring the end from the beginning, And from ancient times things which have not been done, Saying, 'My purpose will be established, And I will accomplish all My good pleasure.'"[22]

God is the Giver/Sustainer of Life

"If He should set His heart on it, If He should gather to Himself His Spirit and His breath, All flesh would perish together, and man would return to dust."[23]

"...then the dust will return to the earth as it was, and the spirit will return to God who gave it."[24]

Our mind cannot conceive higher than God, so by necessity, the highest, most powerful, complete, logical, and excellent view of God that we know is closest to who He is. This will mean that despite all that we do know to be true about God, we will always fall short of our understanding of Him. We will not fully know His ways or grasp what He does. If we can conceive of Him and wrap our minds around Him, that is not *The* God, that is our god.

The God of the Bible declares that He is the final and highest authority. There is no one greater or more powerful, no one more excellent or morally pure, no one else to look to outside of Him. He is "God."

People may call this reasoning into question, but making a defense for "gods" that are subject to others, share their authority, do not

---

22   Isaiah 46:10 (NASB)

23   Job 34:15 (NKJV)

24   Ecclesiastes 12:7 (NASB)

claim ultimate authority, or are akin to an impersonal force or group consciousness is unnecessary because, by their very definition, these gods are not "God" in the classic sense. The thought of God rests on fundamental truths that man has believed from the beginning. In essence, being God means being above all, being beyond measure and compare, and sharing power and authority with no one else. If a "god" does not fit that profile, then by nature he is not God in the classic sense. If one can pass responsibility or power to someone else, then that being is by no means God.

A person who argues against this reasoning or, when one thinks of God, they do not consider Him to have these qualities, they do not have a right to get angry at "god" or call their "god" into question when things do not go their way. If one's god has never claimed ultimate power, authority, goodness, knowledge, etc., then why do they get upset when bad things happen? If their god has these limitations, then they should be at perfect peace when life and its evil and suffering confront them. After all, their god is by nature, limited. To be blunt, they have no reason to ask why God allows evil if they do not hold to this classic view of God.

Man questions God's existence or goodness, especially during pain and suffering, because deep within us, we have certain foundational understandings of God. I am not speaking about religious creations of God but something in our soul that calls us to question when life seems contrary to what it should be. We expect Him to live up to what we innately believe to be true of Him. We have a fundamental expectation of God that is almost universal to all mankind. Because of this, man's anger and confusion arises when evil and suffering happen in this world. It is here at this juncture, where our expectation does not meet our understanding, that doubt, disbelief, rejection, and anger are birthed.

The problem is that we come to this place as a result of a misunderstanding, and this error lies with more than our wrong expectation of how life should work. It deals with almost everything we believe about God and man. Until this changes, in our eyes God will always be on trial. Once we see clearly, it is evident that man, not God, has been the one on trial from the very beginning.

"This power… is infinite. Power in the creature must have limit for the creature itself is finite, but power in the Creator has neither measure nor bound."

C.S. Spurgeon

OUR HISTORY:
WHERE IT ALL BEGAN

"In the beginning, God…"[25]

---

25   Gen 1:1 (NASB)

"History is in fact very useful, actually indispensable…(it) should be studied because it is essential to individuals and to society, and because it harbors beauty…(it) offers a storehouse of information about how people and societies behave…it offers the only extensive evidential base for the contemplation and analysis of how societies function, and people need to have some sense of how societies function simply to run their own lives. History helps us understand change and how the society we live in came to be."[26]

Imagine reading the *Lord of the Rings* saga but starting in the middle of the tale? What important events would you miss that would help you to understand Frodo's quest? The many holes in the story line would make it difficult to get an in-depth picture of the story. You would likely get the gist of the story, but important information about Frodo and the ring would be lost to you. Additionally, relationships between Frodo and Gandalf, or Frodo and Bilbo, would be harder to nail down. You may even misunderstand some of the central characters in the story. As you journeyed alongside Frodo, there would always be some missing background pieces, which would help the story make better sense. Knowing the history would help you sort out and clear up what was missing from your lack of knowledge of the beginning of the story.

This is true of the history of mankind from the very beginning. The less we know about our beginning, the harder it is to get a complete picture of our story. The lack of our primary knowledge of man leads to

---

26   https://www.historians.org/about-aha-and-membership/aha-history-and-archives/his-torical-archives/why-study-history-(1998) Accessed November 2017

a misunderstanding of the main characters that define our story.

The beginning of mankind, written in the Genesis account, explains why we are in our current state. The Genesis account in Scripture has had its share of skeptics and critics. This is not something exclusive to people outside of the church. Over the years, more and more Judeo-Christian religious institutions have distanced themselves or completely abandoned the first account of man and his interaction with God that we find written in Genesis. The problem is that outside of this account, the "why" behind so much of what is wrong in the world and why God permits it does not make sense logically and, even more importantly, theologically. Not only is the Genesis account essential but it is the key to understanding where we are as a people. It identifies the true cause of all that is wrong in this world.

What were the events that took place in creation, and why are they so important to where we are now? The Book of Genesis is fundamental to our understanding of man and his interaction in the world. It is relevant to seeing the larger picture of man's history and putting into focus where and how things went wrong. Without Genesis, so many aspects of God's and man's history become meaningless. Without Genesis, man's picture of God and mankind become confusing and questionable.

IN THE BEGINNING...

From an evolutionary perspective, the narrative of our beginning is based on an analysis of scientific findings of how everything evolved. "A catalyst" caused all that came to be through the process of evolution.

It brought forth planets, stars, and organic matter including early water-based life. Literally every organic object evolved and came forth through this event by utilizing material that was already present in the universe and that existed previously without purpose. This event lacked intelligence, direction, design, and order. It was merely chance + chaos + useful and present material + time to get us to our current state.

In our universe, truths exist that are outside of scientific explanation—philosophical holes for which evolution has no reasonable answer. The existence of the laws of physics, the presence of order and design, the transcendence of truth and logic, and the beginning of organic life—that is, where life came from—cannot be adequately explained by evolution. The existence of the building blocks themselves, which evolutionists theorize brought forth life, are also without explanation. Let me put it this way…if one entered a room and found every part necessary to build a Corvette, and through some random chance, the Corvette actually came together, that person would still have to contend with where the pieces came from in the first place. Regardless of how simple the building blocks of this universe are, their existence still requires an explanation.

Furthermore, without a Creator, there is no logical reason for conscious awareness in life. The fact that we are self-aware is unique and unexplainable. Organic life does not need to be aware to replicate itself. Consider, for example, bacteria, yeast, and fungi. These simple life forms exist without any conscious awareness. The existence of complex, conscious awareness is unnecessary yet awareness is the philosophical component to life. The understanding of "I am" or "he is" exists, but why?

Beauty and love all must have come from a place of thought. Love is not necessary for survival. There are countless creatures that are successful in survival that do not love. They procreate and move on. Why is love present? Beauty is not necessary for survival either. If anything, strength would be more important than beauty. This is evidenced in science and makes sense logically regarding survival; however, beauty does not. Beauty is a soul trait. It captivates the spirit and transcends the physical realm. If evolutionary science wants to say that these all benefit the survival of life, then they have to contend with where the intelligence to know and implement this truth came from. How would an unthinking force know that beauty and love are beneficial for survival, and how would it go about evolving those?

How would an unthinking force know how to self-correct or remove unfit life and keep only beneficial traits? It would need intelligence, wisdom, knowledge and thought to do so. Furthermore, we are created with qualities of the soul that work contrary to evolutionary thought and principle. We have within us the ability to regard and defend life that evolution should technically eradicate. When we personally support the weak, poor, sick, different and vulnerable, we are acting upon that ability. This quality is innate in human beings as it occurs on a global level. It is evidenced individually by one human helping another and globally, by the existence of charities whose sole purpose is to help the most vulnerable and defenseless, seeking to ensure their survival among us. This is an evolutionary contradiction, and as biological creatures on the top of the evolutionary ladder, we should not allow this to be—and yet we do. There are aspects to being human that belong to the soul and are not merely indiscriminate functions of survival, namely—love, hope, compassion, mercy, selflessness, and sacrifice.

Why would a simple life form that exists in an advantageous environment, need to develop into complexity or outside of its beneficial environment? There is zero reason for it to adapt if the environment is ideal. If the environment is such that it necessitates adaptation, then we should argue how it could adapt fast enough to permit the required change. That being said, I am unaware of any true, simple, organic creatures that exist. That is unique, because complexity is a signature of intelligence and thought.

Another challenge to evolution is irreducible complexity. "A system made of several interacting parts, whereby the removal of one part would disrupt the functioning of the whole.... The very structure of these systems—with their interdependent parts working all together or not at all—demands a non-Darwinian, non-chance, non-piecemeal origin."[27] This system stands as an argument against Darwin's quote, "If it could be demonstrated that any complex organ existed, which could not possibly have been transformed by numerous, successive, slight modifications, my theory would absolutely break down."

Consider too that we recognize that Stonehenge, with its simple design, is clearly a product of thought and intelligence. Yet our solar system, which is infinitely far more complex, evolution says was without design. No one would walk up to Stonehenge and assume its

27   http://www.icr.org/article/pseudo-science-attacks-irreducible Accessed October 2018

origin was a random chance; that would be foolish! Yet we are told to believe this about our solar system and our universe. Whether one is considering the crucial placement of the planets, the shape of the orbit, or the order it contains, it is clear that thought and intelligence are behind it. It is like an artist who paints a picture of Denali in Alaska (formerly called Mt. McKinley). We recognize the creative authorship behind the painting but ignore the creative design of the mountain and its surroundings. We accept the intelligence and design in what we create as humans but refuse to acknowledge that a far greater intellect of compounding wisdom, knowledge, power, and intelligence created and ordered the universe.

Let me make it clear; this is an issue of willful rejection and not an absence of proof. As Philosopher Thomas Nagel stated, "I want atheism to be true and am made uneasy by the fact that some of the most intelligent and well-informed people I know are religious believers. It isn't just that I don't believe in God and, naturally, hope that I'm right in my belief. It's that I hope there is no God! I don't want there to be a God; I don't want the universe to be like that. My guess is that this cosmic authority problem is not a rare condition and that it is responsible for much of the scientism and reductionism of our time"[28]

The minute that we recognize authorship in a design of insignificance, the rejection of design in complexity is clearly an issue of choice not truth. Evolutionary answers to some of these questions are philosophical not scientific, yet therein lies its problem. It is not designed to answer questions beyond science alone. It is self-limiting

---

28   Nagel, T. 1997. The Last Word. pp. 130-131

by nature. Evolutionary science is not victorious or complete as it claims to be.

This may not be enough to make the jump from an evolution-directed universe to a God-directed universe, but it is clear that the theory of evolution and how life came to be is not good enough. It offers a theory on how we got here that leaves out the deeper, harder questions like the man behind the curtain in the *Wizard of Oz*, hoping that you do not look at its holes.

If the universe was without life or if that life was without awareness and simple…if universal laws, design, and order did not exist…if life did not move counter to evolutionary principles…if logic were not indeed transcendent…if attributes that are intrinsic to the soul were not present…then maybe evolutionists could have a stronger argument. This is simply not the case.

THEN GOD SAID…

The philosophical opposite to the position of evolution is God. He is the catalyst and the great cause of everything. He is the one who brought forth life, order and design, beauty and love, laws of physics, morality, and logic. God created matter, space, time, and energy. This is the correct view of God, the One powerful enough to bring all into being.

God does not have a beginning. Outside of our want for Him to have a beginning, nothing necessitates that He needs one. Only beings that are created require a beginning. It is as logically simple as that, albeit admittedly still difficult to comprehend. No one can explain how or why this is true, it just is. That being said, it is not illogical or impossible, nor does our lack of understanding remove its truthfulness. Philosophically, this is a place of faith; theologically, it fits the definition of God. Any God that we can comprehend, any God limited or that can be reasoned with or realized, is not God by definition. His greatness attests to His factualness. As Aquinas writes, "…He is the supreme self-subsisting being, and the most perfectly intelligent being."[29]

The very thought of God is scary to a lot of people. He possesses an unrestrainable power and limitless knowledge and wisdom. That is where the problem lies. His supremacy magnifies our inferiority. That being said, it is because of that same wisdom, intelligence, and power that the universe exists. The existence of intelligence, complexity, beauty, order, design, the soul, moral law, personhood, and our awareness can only come from a being greater and more complex than we are. His greatness is to our benefit.

LET THERE BE…

Our beginning is the result of His will. Life was breathed into man and given to beasts. The universe was born from His thought and word. We read that in the beginning, God created the world and its creatures and saw it all as "good." This goodness was an outpouring of His design. This included the original state of man specifically. We were

---

29   Adler, Mortimer. The Great ideas, A Syntopicon 2, Man to World. William Benton, 1952 p. 544

created with moral goodness, beauty, and excellence. This statement should not be glanced over. Everything that comes after the beginning of Genesis will describe God's view of man as being in rebellion, but in the beginning, *"God saw everything that he had made, and behold, it was very good."* So how did we get here?

Good: Adj,

Complete or sufficiently perfect in its kind; having the physical qualities best adapted to its design and use; opposed to bad, imperfect, corrupted, impaired.[30]

---

30   http://webstersdictionary1828.com/Dictionary/good Accessed November 2017

LORA ZIEBRO

THE CHARACTER OF GOD

"God is absolutely good; and so, assuredly, the cause of all that is good."

Walter Raleigh

There are intrinsic truths that we learn about God, His character, and His being from the Genesis account. First, we learn that God is a powerful Creator and a beautiful designer. All that is lovely and wonderful in this world, flows from who He is. Because He is beautiful, powerful, intelligent, personal, and lovely, we are blessed with these attributes in this world. From the expanse of the heavens, the powers of nature, the aroma and healing capabilities of flowers, the uniqueness of wild beasts, the freedom of flying birds, delicious foods, beauty, music, laughter, and love—all that is worthy of admiration in our created world—are from the design of God. That in and of itself is a revelation of God's character. Regardless of whether you believe in Him or not, God's creations are a gift given to man to be enjoyed.

It was after God created the unique person of man that we read, "And God saw everything that he had made, and, behold, it was very good."[31] The culmination of His finished work was before Him, and all that He beheld was good. Man was made different from all that was created, because he was made in God's image. "So God created man in his *own* image, in the image of God created he him; male and female created he them."[32] From the impersonal world to personal man, all was good and reflected God's nature: perfect. God's design of man and this world was free from the unique nature that we call evil. Creation was by its very nature made without any corruption.

In creation, there was a distinct difference between man and all other created works of God. Man was unlike any other creation, in that

---

31   Genesis 1:31 (ESV)

32   Genesis 1:27 (ESV)

he was made in God's image and was given charge over the earth. "So God created man in His *own* image; in the image of God He created him; male and female He created them."[33]

In creation, God gave man

1. The breath of life: man became a living being

2. Personhood: the unique gift of man's human soul

3. A purpose in life: work

4. Relationship and companionship: a helpmate (woman)/friend/ lover to enjoy life with

5. Responsibility and governance: dominion over the world around him

6. Freedom to eat all that is good: enjoyment of the delights of creation

7. Guidance and instruction: including the command to stay away from the one thing that would bring ruin and death

8. Freedom of choice: the Tree of the Knowledge of Good and Evil, and the Tree of Life

9. Personal ownership: ability to name the creatures

10. Himself: a relationship with God

11. His image: ability to create, feel, love, and think

12. Identity: each of us is created distinct and unique

13. Eternal life at his feet: the Tree of Life

---

33   Genesis 1:27 (NKJV)

14. Beauty: the gloriousness of the garden of Eden and the majesty of the heavens

15. His blessing: to be fruitful and multiply upon the earth

All that humans have ever valued, treasured, and longed for was freely provided by God in the beginning. What we strive for and seek now was first gifted. In His wisdom, He designed man, and in His goodness, He gave man everything that would bring joy, meaning, and purpose to his life. His will and desire for man were to live eternally in communion with him. This was His desire for us.

THE FALL: THE OPENING OF PANDORA'S BOX

The fall was a very real event. It is as much a part of the history of man as World War I. Outside of God Himself, there was nothing left unaltered and unaffected from the fall. The greatest change was the entrance of evil into this world. This is when it all began. Adam's choice to rebel against God brought our universal ruin.

Despite this, God's fatherly provision to mankind did not stop after the fall. His care for our condition reached further than our rebellion to Him. While mankind was in a new state of death, with the knowledge of evil and a heart bent toward sin, God personally provided for him. The fall brought an end to the blessing of unbroken fellowship with God, but God was present in rescuing man both physically and spiritually.

After the fall, God

1. Gave mercy: halted the immediateness of death due to sin

2. Made the first sacrifice: God, not man, stepped in to prevent immediate death

3. Provided for man's needs: Clothed Adam and Eve with tunics of skin

4. Demonstrated His justice: made *His* sun to rise on the evil and on the good and sent rain on the just and on the unjust (Matthew 5:45)

5. Guarded man from the Tree of Life (Genesis 3:22): protection from living eternally in a fallen and broken state

6. Gave instruction, direction, and wisdom: ability to govern our life and find our way home

7. Blessed man with a beautiful hope: redemption and forgiveness in Jesus

God allowed man to keep all that was given to him before the fall, with the exception of two things:

1. Our relationship with God was changed.

2. The whole universe developed the corruption from sin.

All of the good that God created was changed into the reality we see now. Like Pandora's box, evil entered the world and poisoned it.

After the fall, the way we related to God and knew Him was forever altered by sin. For the first time, man was faced with an impending judgement. While something was altered, something so beautiful, that showed the depths of God's goodness and love, was given through His Spirit—hope.

THE BEGINNING OF HOPE

"May the God of hope fill you with all joy and peace in believing, so that by the power of the Holy Spirit you may abound in hope."[34]

Hope was birthed in the fall. It revealed that God was not done with this world, or more importantly, that He was not done with man. Hope was created and designed as a beacon to dwell in the imperfect and broken and point us toward wholeness and redemption. Its deep and unexplainable connection to our soul echoes all that should be but was lost due to sin.

This is especially true of our fallen sin nature. Once the soul recognizes the reality of eternity and the impending judgement of sin, the Holy Spirit uses hope to speak peace to our troubled soul as we turn in faith to believe the Gospel.

Hope:

1. Allows us to believe in a real, present, and total mercy for man in Jesus

2. Allows us to see God's mercy for man despite his rejection of God and His ways

3. Frees us to embrace forgiveness and allows us to rest in it

Hope also helps us each day in this broken world. Through it, God speaks to our hearts when we feel we cannot go one more day. It encourages us when the weight of our circumstances are so overwhelming that we can barely breathe. It reminds us that there is

---

34   Romans 15:13 (ESV)

always tomorrow and that we are never truly alone. It reminds man that this life is not all that there is. It is a gift from God to the sinner.

HOPE: EVIDENCE OF GOD

Hope, n., the feeling that what is wanted can be had or that events will turn out for the best.[35]

There are two types of hope that exist in humanity, one is born in the spirit and one comes from the flesh. Hope that stems from the flesh desires the tangible and things of the flesh. Hope born in the spirit stems from the soul. It is a feeling or belief that things will get better. It is this hope, the place of belief, that speaks as evidence of God. It is innate within us, so much so that it is a place where we rest when nothing makes sense around us and everything should cause us to feel the opposite. This hope is God's signature on man's heart. It is an echo of God's goodness. It does not and cannot exist outside of God, because it comes from Him.

By it, we await the future victory over sin and death, and the eventual devastation and permanent extinguishing of evil. It helps us to believe that everything will one day be restored back to God's first design: good.

God created man in goodness and blessed him. He gifted him with beauty, purpose, and love. Once man fell, God rescued man from judgement and granted him mercy and redemption. He instructs, guides, and watches over man daily and blesses him with hope.

---

35   https://www.dictionary.com/browse/hope?s=t Accessed September 2018

Because He alone is good, He gifts man with the ability to share in the overflow of His nature, even after our rebellion. Through His goodness, man's soul is restored.

"Every good gift and every perfect gift is from above, and comes down from the Father of lights, with whom there is no variation or shadow of turning"[36]

---

36   James 1:17 (NKJV)

THE CHARACTER OF MAN

"We have learned to live with unholiness and have come to look upon it as the natural and expected thing."

A.W. Tozer

As with God, Genesis tells us about the character and design of man. We recognize that man is created by God, in His image. To be designed after "God's image" means that man bears a likeness to God in His

1. Mind: reasoning, choice, intellect, ability to create

2. Social and relational composition: community, relationship, emotion

3. Moral makeup: right from wrong, moral compass

That man was made in God's image is unique to all of creation. As Mortimer Adler noted, "The human intellect is able to examine itself. Mind can thus know things about mind which are not otherwise observable"[37] Adler further stated, "Only men can understand as well as perceive; only men can know the universal as well as the particular; only men can think about objects which are neither sensible nor, strictly imaginable—objects such as Atoms and God, the infinite and the eternal, or the intellect itself."[38] However, our likeness is dissimilar to God in that God's character is holy and pure, whereas man's character is presently marked by rebellion and sin.

Our likeness changed in the Garden and continued thereafter. Thomas Aquinas said that man endures a decrease in "his natural inclination to virtue."[39] Adam used the gift of choice to rebel against God. Since then, we have learned a significant truth—that man will

---

37   Adler, Mortimer. The Great Ideas, A Syntopicon 2, Man to World. William Benton, 1952 p 1

38   Adler, p. 5

39   ibid, p. 10

choose rebellion, even when everything else is good. We have seen this same choice repeated in man's history. Instead of praising and worshipping the God who blessed us, we seek our own way and choose rebellion against Him.

Furthermore, when we look at all that was presented to Adam (man) in the Garden of Eden, there is nothing that warranted his rebellion against God. Mortimer Adler summarizes a moment of Milton's *Paradise Lost*, saying it was "the disobedience which results from the disorder of Adam loving Eve more than he loves God."[40] It is quite possible that love was partly behind Adam's choice, but I believe that it was the lie of "something better" that Adam accepted over God's voice. The rebellion began because Adam counted Eve's and Satan's words of more value and worth than God's. It is this same lie that reverberates throughout history until the present time.

Whatever the reason, this one act of choice is the crux of where we are today as a people. This choice to rebel has set the stage for the fallen world that we live in today. After the fall, the world that was created as "good," changed.

The fall brought

1. A curse upon the earth

2. Death into the world: both animals and plants- this point is where the consumption of animals for food began

3. Man's sin nature to man

4. Man's separation from fellowship with the Lord

---

40   ibid, p. 754

5. Evil in this world

6. Death and the inevitable judgement man that will face as a result of his rebellion

Sadly, man has caused the evil that surrounds him. As our years on this earth have passed, we have personally witnessed this truth. For example, in the United States alone in 2017, there was an "estimated 1,247,321 violent crimes that occurred nationwide."[41] The numbers show a corrupted nature present in our society.

Man has repaid God's goodness with

1. Rebellion against His laws, thoughts, and ways

2. Judgement of God's character and His justice over sin

3. Pride: a decision to live life on our terms and be our own god

4. Adultery, spiritual unfaithfulness, and immorality

5. Idolatry: worship and creation of other gods

6. Denial of His existence despite all that points to it

7. Blasphemy: disrespect of His name and holiness

8. Rejection: forsaking God's free gift of forgiveness

While we may blame God for all that is wrong in this world, it is man, not God, who deserves the responsibility. We choose to see this broken, fallen world as a reflection of the character, inconsistency, or failing of God, instead of recognizing the effects and consequences of our sinful life and personal choices. Man wrongs man. As we war for

---

41   https://ucr.fbi.gov/crime-in-the-u.s/2017/crime-in-the-u.s.-2017/topic-pages/violent-crime Accessed 23 October 2018

power, control, money, fame, or lust, we inflict pain on others. Then we get upset when this same pain and suffering is directed toward us or when we have to bear the consequences for our actions.

When people think that man is inherently good, they have to contend with the current state of our sin-filled world, which acts contrary to that thought. To be inherently good means that an essential component of our character and nature would be morally excellent and virtuous, and our actions would reflect that state of being. This reflection would constitute more than man's deeds, because our inherent nature deals with the composition of our soul. The feelings of our heart, the thoughts of our mind, and the words of our mouth speak what composes our soul. Indeed, if goodness were the nature of all humans, our world would reflect that. However, our world reflects a different, inherent nature of man, one of sin and wickedness. The condition of the world does not make sense outside of this truth. Our actions, thoughts and heart validate our fallen nature, and we witness this nature in mankind globally. As long as we deny or reject that it exists, we will always ask "why?" someone acts with evil or feels confused when bad things come our way.

The Christian worldview best describes the world that we live in. It summarizes how we got here, what is wrong with us, and where we go from here. It is a cohesive story that looks clearly and objectively at humanity and answers our most pressing questions.

In the end, it is God's goodness that heals man of this corruption and man who must acknowledge that rebellion exists. When he does,

God is there waiting to restore and to forgive. Those who come to understand this truth come to a place of worship and gratitude for God's mercy and forgiveness, given in spite of our rebellion.

"Though your sins are like scarlet, they shall be as white as snow."[42]

---

42   Isaiah 1:18 (ESV)

FALLEN VIRTUE

"God has chosen the foolish things of the world to shame the wise, and God has chosen the weak things of the world to shame the things which are strong, and the base things of the world and the despised God has chosen, the things that are not, so that He may nullify the things that are"[43]

---

43   1 Corinthians 1:27-28 (NASB)

Moral: Adj

"Relating to the practice, manners, or conduct of men as social beings in relation to each other, and with reference to right and wrong. The word moral is applicable to actions that are good or evil, virtuous or vicious, and has reference to the law of God as the standard by which their character is to be determined. The word however may be applied to actions which affect only, or primarily and principally, a person's own happiness."[44]

Dr. Richard Dawkins found himself embroiled in controversy in 2014 for his comments about whether a woman should give birth to a child with Down Syndrome. A woman on Twitter asked him a hypothetical question about what a woman who is pregnant with a child with Down Syndrome should do. Dawkins tweeted, "Abort it and try again. It would be immoral to bring it into the world if you have the choice."[45] Afterwards, he said in response to his comment:

"If your morality is based, as mine is, on a desire to increase the sum of happiness and reduce suffering, the decision to deliberately give birth to a Down baby, when you have the choice to abort it early in the pregnancy, might actually be immoral from the point of view of the child's own welfare."[46]

Dr. Dawkins declares that his sense of morality is based on a principle: "increasing the sum of happiness and reducing suffering." He also poses an important question by stating **"if"** ("your sense

44   http://webstersdictionary1828.com/Dictionary/moral Accessed November 2017
45   https://www.theguardian.com/science/2014/aug/21/richard-dawkins-immoral-not-to-abort-a-downs-syndrome-foetus Accessed September 2017
46   https://richarddawkins.net/2014/08/abortion-down-syndrome-an-apology-for-letting-slip-the-dogs-of-twitterwar/ Accessed September 2017

of morality is based"). Who or what defines what is moral? By Dr. Dawkins' standards of morality, man should be free to do whatever he wants or needs to guarantee happiness or reduce suffering. For example, terminating a baby merely for having an extra chromosome, leaving one's spouse to have an affair; stealing from one's employer because he makes more money, lying in court to get out of trouble, etc. If happiness is to gain, then moral limitations are irrelevant.

In fairness to Dr. Dawkins, the pursuit of one's happiness (wants, pleasures, way) has been the cause of man's rebellion since the beginning. However, happiness and the removal of suffering are often very selfish ambitions. This would be the case in terminating a child merely because he or she will be born differently or because a parent might have a more difficult job raising that child. It puts the needs of self over the needs of others. This is the complete opposite of a God-centered morality that considers the value of another person as equal importance to oneself.

I AM GOD

"...the serpent told her. For God knows that when you eat of it your eyes will be opened, and you will be like God, knowing good and evil."[47]

Since man has become the sole judge of right and wrong, he has become free to live in accordance with a moral compass that matches his wants and desires. Being subject only to himself and his sense of morality, there is no longer the need for the question, "What has God spoken about this?" or "Is this right?" I believe that these desires are

---

47   Gen 3:4-5 (ESV)

the greatest cause behind man's rebellion. We want the freedom to live as we choose and to be in absolute control over our own life. We do not like being told what to do and having rules placed upon us. This has been the legacy of man since Adam and Eve. It is the signature of the corrupt nature; we want to be God— at least our own god. We would not necessarily say it that way, but it is how we live as a whole. Our morality is driven almost entirely by our thoughts, wants, and necessities.

For instance, a woman is free to leave her husband in pursuit of happiness with another man, because her current marriage brings her "suffering" or "unhappiness" of some sort. The limitations protected under the covenant of marriage and the warnings against divorce and adultery are no longer in place. There is no longer a reason to preserve the marriage either for the betterment of the family or for the promise made under the divine covenant.

THE CONSEQUENCES

As a result, there is no longer the strength forged in marriage that is born from trials, selflessness, perseverance, and forgiveness. There is no longer the discovery that love and lust are different or the learned wisdom that there is growth, depth, and layers to love. There is no longer the understanding that love is indeed a choice. Much is lost from pursuing the temporary and the easy. Mankind loses the mastery of marriage and the depth of real love for the ephemeral and shallow pleasures of the flesh.

The ancient landmarks and teachings are being removed, leaving man to decide morality for himself and to bear the consequences of those decisions instead of heeding the warnings put in place for our protection. We are warned against this in several places in Scripture:

"Do not remove the ancient landmark which your fathers have set."[48]

"My son, do not forget my law, but let your heart keep my commands; For length of days and long life and peace they will add to you."[49]

We are exchanging the wisdom of God for that of man. We see the consequences of this decision in the broken world around us.

The limitations imposed by the divine law of God are guard posts against evil, ruin, and folly. When we remove them, we see the destructive results. A good example is the incremental failure, not success, after breaking the covenant of marriage. "Statistics have shown that in the U.S., 50% percent of first marriages, 67% of second, and 73% of third marriages end in divorce."[50]

Pursuing happiness may appear to bring what is good for us and yet ruin us in the process. Suffering may seem painful and undesirable but can be the very thing that we need the most. This is the wisdom of God.

The divine understanding of good and evil is the bedrock of true morality. Through it, man's awareness of right and wrong is marked clearly before him, and with it, man can escape the pain of ruin and the heartache of sin.

Dr. Dawkins was left to answer the woman within the limitations

48   Proverbs 22:28 (NKJV)
49   Proverbs 3:1-2 (NKJV)
50   https://www.psychologytoday.com/blog/the-intelligent-divorce/201202/the-high-fail-ure-rate-second-and-third-marriages Accessed December 2017

of his atheistic faith. What is amazing about his comment is the why behind having the abortion: "from the point of view of the child's own welfare." Never did it cross his mind that abortion would be far worse for that child than a life with limitations. His suggestion would bring suffering, not end it. It is a shocking statement, because atheists believe that this life is all that there is. It seems more immoral to deny the one chance at life.

Additionally, his atheistic views are inconsistent with the many studies that show how families of children with special needs overwhelmingly believe that their children have brought a positive impact to their lives. His morality can only exist in the shallow temporary, which is why he will never realize the blessing that comes from having a child with special needs.

FIRST-HAND KNOWLEDGE

This is true in my own life. My husband and I are the parents of two beautifully different, wild, and free girls with special needs. My youngest daughter has Down Syndrome, and my oldest daughter has Autism. What I have learned from them is unquantifiable. I know that being their mom has changed my life. I would not be who I am now if not for all my children, but especially these two. It has brought my marriage and family closer and taught us a depth of person and love that we would never have experienced outside of them. Indeed, they are a gift.

I also have learned that difference is a signature of God, not an error. As we read in Exodus 4:11, "*Then the LORD said to him, "Who has made man's mouth? Who makes him mute, or deaf, or seeing, or blind? Is it not I, the LORD?*"[51] His design echoes the beauty of difference and demonstrates His might and artistry. It is man, like Dr. Dawkins, who puts limitations on what is excellent and normal in God's creation. Man sees what has been created differently and chooses what value to place on it, depending on the feelings of the culture and his sinful heart. God sees what He created differently as a way to magnify His name. These are two ways of looking at the same thing.

Anytime we see people with special needs, don't we take notice? Why do we think that these special needs are a bad thing? They are their gift. Their differences allow mankind to stop and think more deeply about life. They are vessels that reflect our humanity, like mirrors held up to our souls. They show what is deepest within us. This is the wisdom of God.

People with special needs are more, not less, and we need to stop listening to foolish people who are led by ignorance and selfishness. The evolutionary principles are wrong. The wisdom that difficulty and suffering breed strength and beauty is lost with atheism, because the wisdom is based on God-centered truth. Outside of God, man will choose abortion to alleviate suffering and miss out on the biggest blessings sent their way.

In the end, if the pursuit of happiness were truly a worthy moral pursuit, it would not harm, rob, destroy, or victimize another person; it would be "moral." However, due to its temporary, carnal, and self-

51   Exodus 4:11 (ESV)

focused nature, this often is not the case. Therefore, happiness is not the measure one should set to define morality. So then, what is?

"Rabbi, who sinned, this man or his parents, that he would be born blind?" Jesus answered, "It was neither that this man sinned, nor his parents; but it was so that the works of God might be displayed in him."[52]

---

52   John 9:2-3 (ESV)

IS IT RELATIVE?

"Tolerance is the virtue of a man without conviction."

G. K. Chesterton

I read an anonymous quote online that said an "atheist is a person who," amongst other things, "believes right and wrong is relative." The idea that right and wrong are subjective, relative, and conditional is growing in popularity and not exclusive to atheists. People find the conditional nature of morality appealing, because it allows man to silence his conscience and ignore warnings of an impending judgement. Those who hold fast to this idea of moral relativism consider those who believe in the absolute nature of right and wrong to be closed-minded. However, in my experience, when I have encountered someone who says that a moral situation is "relative," that person is either neutral to the situation (not the victim/not close to the victim) or does not want to "offend" someone. Anyone arguing that morality is subjective need only to be faced with a cheating partner, the rape of a child, the theft of their property or the murder of a parent. When crime is committed against someone they love, a person knows instinctively that a crime against the soul was committed. There is no reason to argue; it is felt deep within. In that moment, the fixed nature of right and wrong is clear to them.

There are indeed actions that are universally and overwhelmingly accepted as wrong. This truth is understood even by criminals and is the reason why pedophiles are placed in protective custody in prison. "[Child sex offenders] are at risk of being murdered, having their food taken, having their cells defecated and urinated in," said Leslie Walker, a prisoners' rights activist with the Massachusetts Correctional Legal Society. "Their life is truly a living hell."[53] Criminals recognize that

53   http://abcnews.go.com/US/prison-living-hell-pedophiles/story?id=90004
       Accessed June 2016

children being sexually violated is always wrong and never relative.

The absolute nature of right and wrong is true even when behaviors become "common" in the culture. We understand fundamentally that they are wrong and, as such, try to hide them. Let's take adultery, for example. Although movies and television shows tend to glorify it, adultery is not a respectable act. Humans still feel violated when they are betrayed, and people still feel it is wrong to commit adultery. "Ninety-three percent of Americans think being married and having sex with someone else is reprehensible."[54] The view of infidelity as wrong and harmful is not exclusive to marital relationships. In a study conducted to examine the aftermath of infidelity, researchers from the University of Nevada stated, "We know that infidelity is one of the most distressing and damaging events couples face....The person who was cheated on experiences strong emotional and psychological distress following infidelity."[55] The numbers are higher for infidelity in a relationship than in a marriage: "41% of marriages admit to infidelity"; however, "57% of men and 54% women admit to infidelity in any relationship."[56]Despite the culture becoming more tolerant and the more commonplace practice of sexually open relationships, infidelity in a nonmarital relationship is considered inherently wrong and harmful. Both the adulterer and the victim have a shared understanding that something contemptible was done.

---

54   http://i2.cdn.turner.com/cnn/2014/images/01/06/cnn.orc.poll.marijuana.pdf
     Accessed May 2018

55   http://journals.sagepub.com/doi/10.1177/0265407517704091
     Accessed October 2018

56   http://www.statisticbrain.com/infidelity-statistics/ Accessed May 2018

Interestingly enough, in an article titled "The New Monogamy," it was noted that "35 to 55 percent of people having affairs report they were happy in their marriage at the time of their infidelity."[57] This further illustrates that the decision to commit adultery is an act of selfishness and sin, not circumstance or necessity. Adultery is a decision that overwhelmingly rests in desire and lust, because while sex can be an expression of love, sex does not imply love. However, neither desire or lust should govern our commitment to faithfulness. The choice to be unfaithful is a violation of the promise made with someone we share our lives with. It is for this reason that ruin is often the end result. Ironically, "Among people who have admitted to cheating, 64% say that infidelity is always wrong."[58] Their conscience recognizes their sin despite their choice to engage in it.

Society's relaxed views on adultery have not changed the fact of its immorality: "90% of Americans believe it is morally wrong to commit an adulterous act"[59] and "61% would like to see it punished as any other crime."[60] Irrespective of the culture's blasé attitude towards infidelity, its offense is engraved on our souls through God's law: *You shall not covet your neighbor's wife.*[61]

---

57   https://www.psychologytoday.com/us/blog/love-without-limits/201008/the-new-mo-nogamy Accessed October 2018

58   https://www.psychologytoday.com/us/blog/living-single/201010/how-often-do-peo-ple-really-cheat-each-other Accessed October 2018

59   http://www.divorcestatistics.info/latest-infidelity-statistics-of-usa.html Accessed October 2018

60   http://www.divorcestatistics.info/latest-infidelity-statistics-of-usa.html Accessed October 2018

61   Exodus 20:17 (NKJV)

LORA ZIEBRO

MORAL LAW – EVIDENCE OF GOD

The statement that "morality and right or wrong are relative" is an absolute statement. Therefore, it is either true as a whole or untrue as a whole. In order to disqualify an absolute statement, only one point is needed to disprove it, rendering it no longer absolute. In order to prove that morality is indeed objective and not subjective, only one instance where it is universally accepted absolutely is needed. In terms of whether morality is subjective or objective, one needs only to question whether rape would be right in a relative situation? This is asking the question of morality and the standard of its being virtuous, that is, it is good. Let me make that clear, I am not asking do some people feel rape is not bad, but more importantly, when is rape considered innocent and good, ethically? That is a huge distinction. Let me put it another way, when would pedophilia be a good, virtuous, and innocent act?

The only people who would answer this question with a moral affirmative are *possibly* people we put in jail for committing said crimes. We as human beings acknowledge universally that their morals are abhorrent and their behavior perverse. No society anywhere would agree that the rape of a child is morally pure, innocent, or good under any situation.

You may argue that some morality is subjective, but this is a conditional statement and does not encompass the whole of moral law. It is a more reasonable argument, because it acknowledges that there are clear instances where morality is absolute and times where right and wrong is harder to recognize. For example, consider the morality of the

59

death penalty. In this situation, some could rationally argue that the question of good is not clearly defined. However, the nature of good is not in question, but rather the circumstances surrounding it. We are not arguing the quality of good, but whether the death penalty is good.

The nature of good is absolute. It is pure, perfect, and distinguishable. This is why atheists who argue that man can be good (without God) but deny moral absolutes fall into a contradiction. How can one be good (objectively) but have subjective morality? Good cannot be both good and not good or good and up to opinion at the same time and in the same sense. It is against the law of noncontradiction. If good is not good, then it is bad.

THE REAL ISSUE

Rape, adultery, murder, pedophilia, extortion, terrorism, etc. are understood to be universally wrong and only argued as relative by people without the courage to admit that there is a common, moral understanding of this truth. It is indeed not relative, but absolute! However, to acknowledge the universal nature of morality requires man to ask himself how these common laws that govern our life seem imprinted on our soul. Where do they come from? Who gave them to us?

The existence of moral absolutes is evidence that a thinking, personal God exists. They require wisdom and understanding. Furthermore, moral laws stand against the atheistic belief of survival of the fittest in that they regard weakness, imperfection, and disability as qualities to be protected not eradicated. However, to concede here would be to acknowledge the reality of a supreme, moral God. Additionally, it would require us to recognize the existence of laws that are harder to swallow in a culture that accepts the "everything goes" mindset. This is the deeper and real heart of the matter. Not is rape wrong, for only a foolish person would argue that, but more importantly, are things like homosexuality, premarital sex, or abortion wrong? Does a life of sin bring judgement in the end? These are the real questions.

We are so used to the idea of "doing what makes you happy" that we wrongly assume that happiness equates to moral goodness. It does not. In fact, happiness can damage and harm relationships if its pursuit is purely self-focused. Someone can easily behave immorally even if they *feel* it is right. Our hearts do deceive us, as Jeremiah 17:9 states:

"The heart is deceitful above all things, and desperately wicked: who can know it?"

There are fixed laws that exist in this universe: laws that we did not create, we only discovered. Laws, by virtue of their existence, demand a thinking lawmaker. Moral laws are no different. We do not create them; they are fixed within us. This is the purpose and design of our conscience. It is like a compass. It directs us in moral truth and alarms us when something is wrong or when we commit sin. In this way, society may believe a view is antiquated, but man's conscience can still disagree. This "soul" understanding of moral wrong is experiential and evidenced through both feelings and actions on the part of the one committing sin. The person may feel depression, anger, fear, guilt or shame, or they may act with secrecy, addiction, deception, increased rebellion, rejection or avoidance. At times, they may make great efforts to alter the foundations of morality in hopes of silencing the alarm within them. However, while we can numb our conscience to God's laws, we cannot do so completely or erase this knowledge totally. The truth of morality is deeply and profoundly embedded in our humanity. In the end, this very knowledge will stand as our judge.

"They show that the work of the law is written on their hearts, while their conscience also bears witness, and their conflicting thoughts accuse or even excuse them."[62]

---

62   Romans 2:15 (NKJV)

GOOD

"If only it were all so simple! If only there were evil people somewhere insidiously committing evil deeds, and it were necessary only to separate them from the rest of us and destroy them. But the line dividing good and evil cuts through the heart of every human being. And who is willing to destroy a piece of his own heart?"

Aleksandr Solzhenitsyn

BETWEEN GOOD & EVIL

Marcus Cicero stated, *"The function of wisdom is to discriminate against good and evil."* If the purpose of wisdom is to discriminate between these two opposing natures, then it is essential to properly define what qualifies one or the other. What then makes something good or evil?

As humans, we identify good and evil through the actions that display them. However, evil is only recognized when compared with good. It only exists as its antithesis. Without the understanding and knowledge of good, evil would be without definition. As Augustine stated, "Good can exist without evil, whereas evil cannot exist without good."

This also is how we come to know and define morality, as it flows from good and evil. Only by knowing what makes something good or evil can we clearly define what makes something right or wrong. The existence of good and evil makes objective morality factual, because morality cannot be subjective if good and evil exist. This is alluded to in the statement of the opposite by David Silverman, atheist activist and president of American Atheists: "There is no objective moral standard. We are responsible for our own actions...." "The hard answer is it [moral decisions] is a matter of opinion."[63]

In every way, compared with good, evil is its absolute opposite.

---

63   http://religiopoliticaltalk.com/tag/ronald-nash/ Accessed October 2018

- As good creates, evil destroys.
- As good loves, evil hates.
- As good forgives, evil stays bitter.
- As good shows mercy, evil shows cruelty.

- As good heals, evil injures.
- As good sheds truth, evil tells lies.
- As good frees, evil enslaves.
- As good speaks hope, evil speaks despair.

Clearly then, the necessary pursuit is the knowledge of where good comes from and whether a source defines good itself?

To define good and, similarly, to identify what makes something or someone good, one must first use an objective, universal standard to compare: a compass to navigate by. The standard must hold the qualities that are present in the meaning of the understood word. We understand moral goodness, that is, good by quality, to be excellent by virtue, pure by nature, errorless by truth, knowable by thought, and perfect by deed. Those qualities of moral goodness, by necessity, must be inherent and unchanging. Any possibility for change, current existence of variation, or absence of these qualities, would negate its being considered good in substance. There is only One that fits that definition completely and without variation, and that is God, specifically the Judeo-Christian God. We read in Scripture that God is good by nature and thus, embodies the characteristics and quality of good. God is

1. Excellent by virtue: "…for there *is* no iniquity with the LORD our God…"[64]

64 2 Chronicles 19:7 (NKJV)

2. Pure by nature: "You are of purer eyes than to behold evil, and cannot look on wickedness."[65]

3. Errorless by truth: "Every word of God proves true; he is a shield to those who take refuge in him."[66]

4. Knowable by thought: "And this is eternal life, that they may know You, the only true God, and Jesus Christ whom You have sent."[67]

5. Perfect by deed: "As for God, His way is blameless; The word of the LORD is tried; He is a shield to all who take refuge in Him."[68]

6. Changeless: "For I the LORD do not change; therefore you, O children of Jacob, are not consumed."[69]

7. Inherently good by nature: "There is none good but one, that is, God."[70]

Outside of the understanding of good, characterized and identified by God, man really has no basis to define or measure good and evil or right and wrong. As philosopher Richard Taylor stated, "To say that something is wrong because…it is forbidden by God is…perfectly understandable to anyone who believes in a law-giving God. But to say that something is wrong… even though no God exists to forbid it, is not

---

65   Habakkuk 1:13 (NKJV)

66   Proverbs 30:5 (ESV)

67   John 17:3 (NKJV)

68   Psalm 18:30 (NASB)

69   Malachi 3:6 (ESV)

70   Mark 10:18 (NASB)

understandable....The concept of moral obligation [is] unintelligible apart from the idea of God. The words remain but their meaning is gone."[71] God alone brings a surety, clarity, identity, and direction to the necessary questions of right and wrong. C.S. Lewis put it best, "A man does not call a line crooked unless he has some idea of a straight line."

GOOD AS AN ACT / GOOD AS A STATE OF BEING

When discussing the nature of good, it is important to highlight the difference between the act of good and the personal position of good. Good as an act deals with the personal choice of good in a person, specifically, the individual, purposeful choice of good in thought, heart, word, or deed. This act of "good" does not refer to man's individual opinion or shifting moral sense of good. It is an immutable good identified by God's holy standards. Good by act has qualities and characteristics inherent to it: holiness, purity, valor, humility, courage, love, truth, beauty, intelligence, wisdom, knowledge, and selflessness.

Because we are made in the image of God, man can and does do acts of good. However, our good acts will always be marred by our fallen nature and always contain some element of sin. In this way, our fallen acts of good are dissimilar to God's perfect acts of good despite man's being made in His image. The acts of good by God and the acts of good by man are not equal. While we do earthly good and bring forth triumphs and victories against evil, they are inconsistent and can be perverted by motive, moral confusion, variance, perception, emotion, limited knowledge, and sin.

---

71   Taylor, R. 1985. Ethics, Faith, and Reason. pp. 83-84

In contrast, God has an excellence and mastery of good by choice, because "good," by design, is an outpouring of the nature of God. God possesses all the inherent qualities of good in excellence without the marring of evil, because God's nature is altogether absent of evil. Additionally, God's acts of good are unaffected and unperverted by man's opinions, emotion, desire for acceptance, pursuit of the temporary, and striving for power and money. His excellence of good deals with the total of all knowledge, of all things, over all time, that He alone is privy to.

Good as a state of being is positional. It deals with the nature of good in a person. When speaking of good in respect to God, we must look at more than the positional quality of God, because the nature of good is an outpouring of who God is. Good does not make God, God makes good. Good is who He is. He embodies, identifies, gives meaning to, and constitutes good. Without God, good would not exist. As a result, God cannot do evil, because the total of His nature is good without the presence of even the smallest degree of evil. He alone has a good nature completely and in totality: thoughts, heart, word, and action. Due to this, He alone can do purely good acts. "Good" is good, because God is good.

GOOD WITHOUT GOD

The popular atheist slogan "Good without God" makes an interesting claim, but can man truly be good without God? As stated earlier "to *be* good" deals with the nature of man, not his acts. It is an understanding of the complete person—mind, body, and soul, with a nature of good in total and without error or marring. No man has this nature. No man is good by nature even with God, let alone good without God. All men possess corruption, as is evidenced in the world around us. Only one man has ever lived who had the quality of good in His being, and that is Jesus Christ.

While good is not our nature as humans, God has given man the ability to know, experience, and do good, humanly speaking. It is a gift to the earth that God has given man the ability to draw, teach, preserve, encourage, and protect himself. In this way, man can *behave* in a "good" way and *do* good deeds and not necessarily believe in God. But man cannot *be* good, with or without God. This is an important distinction. It also is important to point out that without God as the standard of good, the parameters that constitute good become blurred and begin to crumble. It becomes subject to opinion, error, emotion, pressure, culture, and power. As philosopher Julian Baggini stated, "If there is no single moral authority [that is, if there is no God, then] we have to in some sense 'create' values for ourselves…that means that moral claims are not true or false in the same way as factual claims are… moral claims are judgments [that] it is always possible for someone to disagree with…without saying something that is factually false…you may disagree with me but you cannot say I have made a factual error."[72]

In some ways, when people argue morality without God, it is a moot point. The framework for morality has already been established on the shoulders of religion. All that is now done is a tweaking of morality. Mankind already has the bedrock of morality imprinted in

72   Baggini, J. 2003. Atheism: A Very Short Introduction. pp. 41-51

them by God and witnessed through our cultural knowledge of right and wrong, which claims its origins from religious tenets, laws, and traditions. To put it bluntly, morality belongs to the religious! Any understanding or choice to adhere to moral principles is still based on a foundation already laid—a structure whose boundaries and parameters are established by and through God. Being "good" is then being obedient in action to those set parameters and being bad is their rejection. The parameters, however, are already set.

Furthermore, while modern man easily has an awareness of morality, we would not *know* morality, apart from God. Think through what we know to be true about morality. It often is contrary to primal responses. Take lying, for example. In terms of a purely primal action, lying to obtain something I need is sensible. However, lying is known to be morally wrong. Man would not naturally conceive of this on his own. We do not naturally hold true to this law as a people; therefore, it would be reasonable for us to believe that lying is right. Yet despite how often man lies, *we know it to be true,* that lying is wrong.

If you take most of the laws given in the second part of the ten commandments, the section that deals with man's relation to man, we see this same contradiction of normal instincts. We are told not to steal, commit adultery, or covet what is not ours. We still place these biblical principles as moral standards regardless of how natural they are or how often we do it. It is a contradiction of self and does not serve our regular tendencies. Why would man create them as they work against our nature? Yet, they exist. This could be said for many of the moral truths we believe as humans.

By design, evolution is immoral. It demands no justice and considers no law. It holds no one accountable and shows neither favor to the just nor judgement to the unjust. The act of evolution honors the violent and the brutal as champions of survival. It is unmoved by plights of compassion, the needy, the sick, and the helpless. It is indifferent to compassion, hope, and purpose. It has zero regard for the humanness of the soul. It is silent to the cries at night. It forgets and erases heroes, victories, and triumphs into the vastness of inevitable time. Like the dust, they are all equally forgotten. It has one thought in its focus: survival, by any means necessary. It is selfish by nature as it should be, with it being void of spirit and soul.

There is no good or evil or morality in evolution, only time and survival.

Atheists who desire to be "good without God" want the claim of good, because the truth of atheism is disturbing to the conscience. Adopting morality is more palatable. In this way, they can ignore the reality that brute survival, amongst other things, denies every man their intrinsic value and the essence of the soul. It steals something distinct from God, that is, good, to quiet the deadness, immorality, and hopelessness that marks it.

Can people really be "good without God?" No, they cannot. How would they even begin to define good to answer this question? Without God they cannot define the nature of good or evil or the moral obligations that characterize them. This leads me to my last point.

While man does not have an inherent nature of good, man can

71

be made good by God. Our nature becomes one of a redeemed sinner with a righteousness or goodness that is not our own. Christians call it imputed righteousness. It is a goodness that comes through Jesus. He takes and pays man's total debt of sin, rendering him free from the penalty of crimes against God and man. In exchange, He gives man His own goodness. So we are neither sinful nor neutral before God, but rather, we are made perfect in, by, and through Jesus. This is the only circumstance in which man is good by nature; however, that nature is gifted to Christians by faith in Jesus Christ alone. So, it is not that we by our own nature become good, but rather by having God's nature become good.

GOOD AS AN OUTCOME

"Yet you have not returned to me."[73]

I believe that in order to really understand good we must consider two things: its earthly objective, and whether God's idea of good is deeper and broader than our own.

Our idea of good is limited to this earthly realm, and we define it based on earthly things. Hence, when we consider it, we consider it by temporal boundaries. Mankind defines good almost exclusively by his experience in life and how he views the world around him. Often, we look at "the good life" and "good living" to identify, define, and compare what is good in our own lives. Conversely, we attach pain, suffering, and difficulty to what is wrong or evil. If this life were all that there is, then it would be reasonable to assign good and evil in this way.

---

73   Amos 4:6 (NKJV)

However, if this world is meant to be a temporary dwelling for us, then good needs to be understood in consideration of the eternal. It is clear in Scripture that where we spend eternity is of absolute importance to God. As we read in 2 Peter 3:9, *"The Lord is not slack concerning His promise, as some count slackness, but is longsuffering toward us, **not willing that any should perish** but that all should come to repentance."*[74] In this way, for God, good lies beyond finite qualities.

GOOD'S PURPOSE

There is both an earthly and heavenly purpose for good. The earthly purpose of good serves man on many different levels. For example, good helps us to establish law by which we can govern and live with order and rule. By it we understand right and wrong, which allows us to live in community while we are on this earth. It helps us to recognize its opposite: evil, and acts of evil. This of course helps us to define, identify, and distinguish evil and gives us the desire to fight against it when we see it. By good, we know love, beauty, comfort, and warmth, and we feel "good" in moments of laughter, forgiveness, and peace. Good also drives us to protect, to defend, and to cherish. These are some earthly applications and reasons for good.

There also are heavenly reasons for good. Good helps us to understand God and His nature and commands. By it, we can better know who we are and how our lives and actions relate to God. Good is like a measuring stick, showing us God's holiness and character and where we stand as people before Him. It shows us how we stack up to

---

74   2 Peter 3:9 (NKJV)

God's laws, which point to our sin, directing us to the understanding of our need for a Savior. Good reminds us that this world is broken, and it encourages us to not make this world our sole ambition. It points us toward a better tomorrow and the promises of eternal life where "pure goodness" exists without corruption.

God's purpose also is to bring us to a place of surrender and repentance so that we may inherit eternal life. In this way, good is sometimes painful or unpleasant. God's heavenly purpose for good protects man from the illusion that this world is all that there is and directs us toward a heavenly home. This is God's desire for all mankind. It was this way from the beginning when He made a perfect garden so that man could walk with Him and know Him. His desire for us has not changed. What has changed is our state before Him: one of rebellion and transgression.

As a result of God's priority for man's eternal soul over man's temporal happiness, I believe that God allows trials and difficulties to enter man's life directly. We see God's corrective hand over His creation and, most especially, over His children. Trials, consequences, suffering, and heartache are tools used to break man from the danger of a life of immorality and sin. They are also used to warn and awaken man from the belief that this world is all that there is. While painful, they are used to help someone in repeated, unrestrained, unrepentant rebellion, and sometimes they are the only means capable of breaking us from being under the allure of this temporary world. In Scripture, these measures were used only after warnings and calls to repent were consistently ignored and disregarded. God's purpose in those sufferings was restoration. Those moments of great trial were a consequence of man's rebellion against God and not a result of some indifferent, cruel punishment.

It is easy for a person who is trying to find a problem with God to call His methodology into question. However, many parents are familiar with making "tough love" decisions for children who refuse to make good decisions or those who continue to go into criminal, damaging, and addictive behavior in spite of repeated warnings, chances, and pleadings. Ignoring or consenting to that behavior can bring ruin, whereas pressure and discipline can be restorative. There are homes, rehabs, camps, scared straight programs, etc. that exist because some people will not make "right" choices without pressure or punishment. After parents try the grace-and-mercy approach, sometimes the only option is discipline. In the following scriptures, we see examples of these moments of discipline and the outcome desired by God. Many times, despite the pressure of these circumstances, Israel still rejected God. These times did, however, bring the necessary humbling that eventually led the way to true repentance.

"O LORD, are not Your eyes on the truth? You have stricken them, but they have not grieved; You have consumed them, but they have refused to receive correction. They have made their faces harder than rock; **They have refused to return.**"[75]

"And you shall remember that the LORD your God led you all the way these forty years in the wilderness, **to humble you and test you**, *to know what was in your heart, whether you would keep His commandments or*

75   Jeremiah 5:3 (NKJV)

not. **So He humbled you,** *allowed you to hunger, and fed you with manna which you did not know nor did your fathers know,* **that He might make you know that man shall not live by bread alone;** *but man lives by every word that proceeds from the mouth of the LORD. Your garments did not wear out on you, nor did your foot swell these forty years.* **You should know in your heart that as a man chastens his son, so the LORD your God chastens you.**"[76]

We must pause here and remember that we overwhelmingly tend to forget God when things are "good" and when we are in a place of peace and ease. The better our circumstances are and the more we think we know, the more we reject God. We feel that we no longer need Him, so we no longer seek Him. This often happens in human relationships. Relationships fall into indifference and complacency only to be awakened by relational difficulty. We tend to "forget" our role in maintaining a healthy relationship until problems arise or until it is too late. We see this truth and reminder echoed throughout Scripture.

"*Why should I pardon you? Your sons have forsaken Me and sworn by those who are not gods.* **When I had fed them to the full, they committed adultery and trooped to the harlot's house.**"[77]

"**Beware that you do not forget the Lord your God** *by not keeping His commandments, His judgments, and His statutes which I command you today, lest—* **when you have eaten and are full, and have built beautiful houses and dwell in them; and when your herds and your flocks multiply, and your silver and your gold are multiplied, and**

---

76   Deuteronomy 8:2-5 (NKJV)

77   Jeremiah 5:7 (NASB)

all that you have is multiplied; when your heart is lifted up, and you forget the Lord your God who brought you out of the land of Egypt, from the house of bondage."[78]

With humans, the worst that can happen is the end of a relationship or the breaking up of a family. However, for man and our relationship with God, our worst consequence is eternal punishment. *"The wicked shall return to Sheol, all the nations that forget God."[79]* and *"for the Lord knows the way of the righteous, but the way of the wicked will perish."[80]*

When we consider that God's purpose for man lies beyond the earthly realm, and the Lord knows that all man's works will be accounted for on the Day of Judgement, we can appreciate why God does not want man to face that fate. God's desire is to prevent the spiritual death of man's soul, knowing this death is an everlasting one. Good here is not limited to our time on earth. It also considers the outcome of our soul.

"And this is the will of him who sent me, that I should lose nothing of all that he has given me, but raise it up on the last day"[81]

---

78   Deuteronomy 8:11-14 (NKJV)

79   Psalm 9:17 (ESV)

80   Psalm 1:6 (ESV)

81   John 6:39 (ESV)

EVIL

N / E'VIL

Evil is natural or moral. Natural evil is anything which produces pain, distress, loss, or calamity or which in any way disturbs the peace, impairs the happiness, or destroys the perfection of natural beings.... Moral evil is any deviation of a moral agent from the rules of conduct prescribed to him by God, or by legitimate human authority; or it is any violation of the plain principles of justice and rectitude.... All wickedness, all crimes, all violations of law and right are moral evils.... Depravity; corruption of heart, or disposition to commit wickedness; malignity.[82]

---

82   http://webstersdictionary1828.com/Dictionary/evil Accessed June 2016

EVIL IS REBELLION

Evil is complex. This is especially true when people try to define evil outside of a God-centered understanding. It is too simplistic to say that it is merely the absence of good, although that is true of evil. Evil can be manifest in an act, choice, thought, state of being, or spirit. In its active state, in relation to God and man, evil is a personal rebellion against God, His character, and His laws.

The act of disobeying God—which is sin, no matter how small and insignificant we believe it to be—is an act of treason, contempt, and betrayal. It is an act of evil, because it is a rebellion against good. Furthermore, God has provided man with good, and man has repaid that good with defiance. Psalm 145:9 says, "The LORD is good to all: and his tender mercies are over all his works." Our sin becomes not just a breaking of the law but also a personal, individual offense against the person and nature of God— one that is unwarranted in every way. In this way, our rebellion is magnified, because it is against innocence.

This is compounded by man's further choice to reject God and embrace idols that are void of power, inferior in character and goodness, and only exist in our own minds. Idolatry to God is similar to adultery to man. It is an act of cheating and a violation of a relationship. This is the point behind scriptures that state that God is a jealous God. We give to another the affection and worship that belongs to Him alone. Humanly speaking, it is like a wife who cheats on her husband while he is on a business trip. No one is emotionless to an unfaithful spouse, and God is no different. In this way, jealousy is not sin. It is not an act of lust over something one wants that is not theirs, but an act of grief over something that is rightly theirs but has been given to another. This is righteous jealousy.

Lastly, evil is to reject God's gift of forgiveness in Jesus while seeking to bribe him with something lesser in value, purpose, and goodness, that is, our good works and our own way. This indeed is its own evil, because we assume that what we bring to God is of greater value or worth than the sacrifice of His own Son and has greater warrant than what has already been decided by God. It is a threefold offence. It is a rejection of God's plan and a rejection of God's Son, and it involves the sin of pride that assumes our idea to satisfy the debt we owe is better than His. Anytime we feel that what we offer to God is of greater importance than the life of His Son, we have entered into the sin of pride.

EVIL AS AN ACT / EVIL AS A STATE OF BEING

When looking at evil, it is important to differentiate between evil as an act and evil as a state of being. Evil as an act deals with man's individual, personal choices. In this circumstance, one can find presumably "good" people doing "bad" things, such as committing brief, impulsive, or self-destructive acts of crime, immorality, and other types of sin. This is where heinous and incomprehensible acts are seen. Crimes that are premeditated, grossly immoral, confusing, and shocking. This is where the "choice to act" shows itself most. Sin can be committed by the religious and the non-religious alike, as we see with David and Bathsheba. People can go as far into evil or be as far removed from it as their personal choices and desires lead them.

Evil as an act is a violation and a rebellion against good. An evil act can be passive or active. If, for example, I watch someone commit a crime and do not do anything, or if I am silent when I know someone is being unfairly and wrongly accused, I would be passively participating in evil. If I personally and knowingly partake in the crime, that would clearly be active evil. These passive and active acts violate another person and violate "good."

IS MAN INHERENTLY GOOD?

Evil, as a state of being, is positional. It deals with the corrupted nature of the person. It affects the whole of man: thoughts, mind, heart, and action. This position is our nature as human beings after the fall, and the sins we commit extend from this nature. Because evil is present and accessible within us, we merely act upon it. This is why we need spiritual renewal.

There are those who disagree with the belief that man has a corrupted nature. They believe that man is inherently good; however, one cannot be inherently good and at the same time perform immoral deeds. The very fact that man does even one immoral deed disqualifies him from being inherently good. The two are contradictory. This is important to understand, because while one may not consider man to have a corrupt nature, man can only take part in what is present within him. If evil were not present, man could not partake in it. Evil is not natural or normal, it is an aberration.

The act of evil can be restrained, controlled, and subdued, but the evil nature always exists. As humans, we face this truth every day. It is why immorality, addictions, and bondages have such power over us and why they tempt us so much. This is why it is so important for us to have safeguards that keep us from making dangerous decisions. This quote from secular atheist Ta-Nehisi Coates is a great illustration of this truth: "I've been with my spouse for almost 15 years. In those years, I've never been with anyone but the mother of my son. But that's not because I am an especially good and true person. In fact, I am wholly in possession of an unimaginably filthy and mongrel mind. But I am also a dude who believes in guard-rails, as a buddy of mine once put it. I don't believe in getting 'in the moment' and then exercising willpower. I believe in avoiding 'the moment.' I believe in being absolutely clear with myself about why I am having a second drink, and why I am not; why I am going to a party, and why I am not. I believe that the battle is lost at Happy Hour, not at the hotel."[83]

The sin nature exists within all mankind. Nothing natural can tame it totally. It needs to be put to death and reborn to a new life. In doing so, man's positional nature is restored from one of corruption to one of virtue. This is one of the outcomes of salvation in Jesus.

Although there is still the possibility of performing singular acts of evil after salvation, this will no longer be the course or outcome of the person's life. The nature of the man has changed, and as a result, his choices also will change. It may be slow at first, similar to how a

---

83   https://www.theatlantic.com/national/archive/2012/12/violence-and-the-social-compact/266514/. Accessed June 2017

child grows and learns to become an adult, but in time there will be a recognizable difference from who they were before.

This change will affect the whole person and would be seen in both their public and private life. If they do not bear the fruit of a changed nature, or if that change is only in the public eye and in private they are no different than they ever were, there is reason to doubt the genuineness of their salvation. I make this caveat between the public and private life, because the fraud is most evident to those who know them privately.

As a final point, the positional nature of God is the reason why He cannot do evil. God is, by nature, altogether good. Evil does not exist within Him, so He cannot partake in it. He is, by nature, free from it completely. It is why, in reference to good, there is only One who is good, and He is God.

EVIL AS A SPIRIT

It is important to mention that evil exists as a spirit. The Bible warns about the being called Satan and his influence on the earth. Satan is a personal, individual being whose nature is the farthest from God. He is altogether void of all that is good. The Bible calls him a thief, the father of lies, and a murderer, among other things. Of Satan, we are told:

"Be sober, be vigilant; because your adversary the devil walks about like a roaring lion, seeking whom he may devour."[84]

---

84   1 Peter 5:8 (NKJV)

"You are of your father the devil, and you want to do the desires of your father. He was a murderer from the beginning, and does not stand in the truth because there is no truth in him. Whenever he speaks a lie, he speaks from his own nature, for he is a liar and the father of lies."[85]

Satan is separate from us, but we share in his corrupt nature. As a result of this shared nature, he can and does influence man. While his power is limited and temporary, his works are present on this earth. Additionally, we are told in Scripture that Satan is not the only evil spirit. Scripture states that there is an army of evil spirits that man can wrestle with: *"For our struggle is not against flesh and blood, but against the rulers, against the powers, against the world forces of this darkness, against the spiritual forces of wickedness in the heavenly places."*[86]

The person of Satan and his presence on the earth plays an active part in the condition and state of the world. Unfortunately, as our culture dismisses the belief in God, we also dismiss belief in Satan and evil spirits. This leaves man vulnerable to satanic attacks levied at him. We are cast into wars that affect what is most precious to us: our souls, our marriages, our families, and our purposes. All of this can take place without the knowledge of who we are at war with.

Because we have chosen to believe that Satan does not exist, he becomes an effective adversary. My favorite line from the movie *The Usual Suspects* is, "The greatest trick the devil ever pulled was to convince the world he didn't exist." How true this is! We explain away the presence of Satan, looking for any answer but the biblical one. Still,

---

85   John 8:44 (NASB)
86   Eph 6:12 (NASB)

he is active in the world, and his influence is far reaching. We are all involved in a war that surrounds us. Knowing that our enemy exists will prepare us to get into our own fight.

Evil is impossible to fully understand outside of the biblical sense. The best attempts to do so will be imperfect and generic, living in the world of the "possible" and "probable" but never becoming anything more than assumptions and best guesses. It will always fall short of the true nature and understanding of evil, because it refuses to consider the source and origin of evil himself (Satan). John Wesley said it best, "… There is no evil done, or spoken, or thought without the assistance of the devil, who worketh with strong though secret power in the children of unbelief. All the works of our evil nature are the work of the devil."

EVIL AND GOD'S LAW

"Children begin deceiving their parents as early as 6 months of age. Dr. Vasudevi Reddy of the University of Portsmouth identified 7 types of deception used by toddlers based on studies of 50 children and interviews with parents. For some, the deception began at 6 months with behavior, such as pretend laughter or crying when nothing was wrong just to get attention."[87]

Humans are profoundly aware of their sin. Even from a young age, we know when we are doing something wrong. For those who have been around a young child long enough, this truth is plainly evident. Children will sneak around to get what they want after they have been

---

87   http://liespotting.com/2010/06/10-research-findings-about-deception-that-will-blow-your-mind/. Accessed June 2017

told "no" by their parents. They know that to get what they want, they must do so without their parents' knowledge. In other words, they know they must be deceptive. Of course, deception in a child is different from deception in an adult, but the awareness is there either way.

The knowledge of sin is evidenced in actions such as lying, scheming, secrecy, sneaking, and manipulation. The very nature of these acts show that the person is cognizant that they are doing something they should not be doing. We hide things that we do not want people to know about us, things we are ashamed of, and things that are wrong, all as an active response to our acknowledgment of guilt. We see this conscious understanding of right and wrong in Romans 2:14-15, *"for when Gentiles, who do not have the law, by nature do the things in the law, these, although not having the law, are a law to themselves, who show the work of the law written in their hearts, their conscience also bearing witness, and between themselves their thoughts accusing or else excusing them."*

While man is fully aware of his sin, when considering God's law man tends to diminish and justify wrong. It is easy to recognize sin in another person, but when looking at ourselves, we minimize it. In the same way, it is easy to recognize gross immorality and acknowledge that it deserves a punishment; however, we do not see "common" sin as worthy of the same penalty. As a result, we do not see our guilt before God's law. There is an assumption that God only sees heinous sins as worthy of judgement. This belief allows man to think that as long as we do not commit grave acts of sin, we do not need to be afraid of punishment from God. By avoiding grave acts of sin, we are essentially "good" before God. We can easily agree that a murderer deserves to be punished, but we do not believe that we deserve to be punished for lustful thoughts.

While not everyone is guilty of the act of murder, everyone is guilty of common or daily sins, such as lying. When I have spoken to people about lying being a sin, they often justify themselves by saying that "Everybody lies." This response shows several things:

1. The universal nature of the sin

2. The universal guilt of all men

3. The universal knowledge of man's guilt

4. How much people minimize its gravity due to being desensitized from it

The problem with this last point is that the question is not about the sheer amount of people who lie, but specifically, is lying wrong?

IS WRONG ALWAYS WRONG?

Lying is commonly justified by giving "acceptable" and "excusable" reasons to lie. One hears responses like, "It was just a white lie" or "It didn't hurt anyone," but having an excuse has nothing to do with actual guilt of wrong. The only question that matters is whether the offense is condemned by the law. We see this truth illustrated in Proverbs 6:30-31: *"Men do not despise a thief if he steals to satisfy himself when he is hungry; But when he is found, he must repay sevenfold; He must give all the substance of his house."* While it is clear that the man stole

88

for "understandable" reasons, the law "Thou shalt not steal!" was still broken. As a result, a thief must still pay a debt to satisfy the law.

Because daily offenses like lying are common and man has become so desensitized to them being wrong, man minimizes his guilt and no longer recognizes his criminality. We see the offense in gray areas, not in black and white. We also look at our guilt on a curve by comparing our actions to others around us. Furthermore, we consider our motivations, and then we judge our guilt against them. However, all of these have no bearing on the Law.

MAN'S THOUGHT

The Lie	The Why	Did you lie?	Broke the law?
"No, you don't look fat in that dress!"	Didn't want to get in an argument.	Yes	No

REALITY: THE LAW WAS BROKEN

The Law is holy, eternal, and absolute, and the punishment for breaking the law is set. The Law says, "*You shall not bear false witness (lie) against your neighbor.*"[88] It's black and white. The punishment set for breaking the Law is also black and white: "*...and all liars shall have their part in the lake which burns with fire and brimstone, which is the second death.*"[89]

I watched a video about a woman who went before a judge because

---

88   Exodus 20:16 (NASB)
89   Revelation 21:8 (NKJV)

she owed several parking debts to the city. She explained to the judge that there were factors that came into play, specifically her son's dying the previous year. The judge heard her "why" but still ruled that she was guilty of breaking the law and had to pay a fine. The judge heard the woman's circumstances and considered them in his final sentence. He found her guilty and ordered her to pay a fine. Guilty, yes. Fine, yes. Afterwards, out of his kindness, he granted that her fine be completely eliminated, but only after the law was ruled upon and her guilt was established. While mercy was granted, the law was still enforced. His mercy and compassion toward her and her circumstances had nothing to do with her guilt.

Now imagine standing before a Judge who knows all the inner workings of your heart, mind, and actions. The Judge in this courtroom is omniscient and not limited as human judges are.

This is the predicament; the Judge knows the real "why" behind our motives. He indeed knows our hearts. He knows every time and instance we have thought, felt, said, or have done wrong. He knows the deepest and truest reasoning behind every choice we make or thought we think. He is aware of the real motivation behind the explanations that we give to others and the excuses that we offer that make us look good. He is aware when a man who has been asked by his wife how she looks in a particular outfit is untruthful because he does not want her to feel bad or because he is self-focused and wants to avoid an argument. In matters of the Law, even in our human courts, lying is a crime against the Law. Period!

Let me make it clear that I am not advocating that a man should be unkind or hurtful in his response to his wife. I would certainly argue that there is wisdom in using the right words when put in a delicate situation, especially in matters of the heart. What I am trying to show is the power behind the law. It stands as a judge against sin. This is why the cross is man's only hope. At the Cross, the exactness of the Law is met with the mercy of the Lawgiver. In this way, holiness is not compromised, but neither is love. On the cross, the judgment and penalty are still levied and paid by Jesus' death, but they are met with His act of supreme selflessness, mercy, and sacrifice for those who believe in Him.

God also rules against crimes of the law that are hidden. By this, I mean the offenses of the heart and mind; for example, if one feels hate (1 John 3:15), jealousy (Mark 12:31), lust (Matthew 5:28), rebellion (1 Samuel 15:23), if one gossips (Titus 3:2, Leviticus 19:16), is silent in evil (Psalm 94:16), or enjoys wickedness (3 John 1:11); etc. All of these are offenses against God's Holy Law and are acts of evil. They are crimes:

1. Against the Law of God

2. Against the person of God

3. Against other men

All of them have a fine. This is no different than any other courtroom on earth where man's law is broken. The only difference is that on the day that we face the Judge, all of the offenses from our life here on earth, both hidden and visible, will be brought before an all-knowing, all-seeing, holy and honest Judge.

"Therefore, to him who knows to do good and does not do it, to him it is sin"[90]

---

90   James 4:17 (NKJV)

THE LAW OF LOVE

"Above all, keep loving one another earnestly, since love covers a multitude of sins."[91]

---

91   1 Peter 4:8 (ESV)

I must pause here and go deeper into God's Law to discuss the Law of Love. Without an understanding of the law of love, Christianity appears one-dimensional and indifferent to the frailty of man, our humanness as imperfect creatures, and circumstances beyond our control. It also would appear ignorant to men who heed the letter of the law but have wickedness deep within them. However, God is uniquely aware of and remembers all these things.-

Man is judged by the exactness of the law together with the law of love. The law of love exposes those who have a genuine faith in God and, conversely, those who play religion or wield it as a sword for power and control. This was part of the issue that Jesus had with the religious rulers of His day. He saw men who obeyed the law but only superficially. These were the "taste not, touch not," "wear this not that" religious people. They were secret offenders of the same laws that they judged others so harshly by. They were men who had no place for mercy despite desperately needing their own. When love came into play, they were fully void of it. It was this very thing that exposed their separation from God.

This is still true today. Many people speak about the law and speak about God, but their hearts are cold and wicked. They fill churches, preach sermons, perform ministry, have a visible obedience, and tithe regularly, but deep within they are just playing religion.

THE ILLUMINATOR

The law of love does not nullify the Holy Law. On the contrary, it magnifies and illuminates it. This is the difference between looking at a beautiful picture of an ocean and personally standing before that same ocean. As one takes in the different colors, hears the layers of sound, sees the movement of the waves, feels the texture of the sand, and watches the life that is within it, they recognize that a picture is beautiful, but the actual ocean is maximally more so. The picture is merely a glimpse of something so fundamentally more profound and deep. The law is no different. It is a picture of something more immeasurably beautiful: the holiness of God and the power of His love.

The law is meant to expose what is deep in man. Here, Jesus speaks beyond adultery to lust, and beyond murder to hate. The holy law looks at a person's choice, while the law of love looks at the person's motive, his why—they work in concert. We are told in Scripture to love the Lord **and** obey His law (Deuteronomy 10:12, 11:1).

The law of love sheds light on both God's and man's character. It was demonstrated by Jesus many times in Scripture, and, to this day, it has become a stumbling block for the religious and powerful. Jesus showed that the strength of the law encompassed, not excluded, love and mercy as seen in John 8:1-11. The cross itself was the greatest demonstration of love in the history of mankind.

The Bible repeatedly commands us to: "love the Lord your God…" "love your neighbor as yourself," "the greatest of these is love," "love covers a multitude of sins," love one another," etc. The principles of this law is the cornerstone of the cross and redemption. Due to this law, man can and does receive mercy and forgiveness despite being in rebellion and deserving punishment.

LOVE COMPELS

The law of love compelled Jesus to die on the cross for sinners. The law of love drove the Father to provide a way for man to be forgiven through Jesus. The law of love opened the door of forgiveness as God Himself demonstrated the perfect working of this love, laying down what was most precious to Him: His Son. The law of love moved Jesus to sit with the outcasts, the marginalized, and the sinners.

The law of love beautifully clarifies the Holy Law by going deeper into the spirit, mind, and heart of man. When man is found guilty before God, it is an absolute and complete guilt. This is important, because the consequences of violating the law are eternal.

The exactness of the law is why Christ had to die to free man, but the law of love is why Christ chose to die to free man. This is one way that Christianity is unique from all other belief systems. Jesus goes beyond words and defines love for us. He enters the world of sin and death to bring home those most worthy of death, due to their sin. The law of love proceeds from the purity of holiness and perfection within the Father. It beckons man to come and be reconciled and healed.

GOD IS LOVE

Scripture tells us that God is love, not merely that God loves, but that God *is* love. Within Him, as His being, He is love. Love is an evidence of God. It does not come from emptiness. It has to proceed from one thing and be given to another. What it proceeds from must have it within itself. When we hear that God is love, we understand that it is He who brings forth love.

Love is a fundamental characteristic of the Christian gospel. While religion overwhelmingly emphasizes righteousness by works, the center of Christianity deals with righteousness by faith, driven by the love of a holy God. Christianity is uniquely centered around mankind bearing God's mark of love, the cross, on our souls. We are known and identified by this mark. This love is the highest demonstration ever witnessed in creation. A place where the most precious was given for the most beggarly.

This is evidence of Christianity's truth. Religious works can be obeyed and demonstrated externally, yet still allow for sin to reign in the soul. Christianity calls men to deep confession of the soul, ripping off every layer of sin and rebellion and leaving no part unexposed. There is no lie unseen, no hate unknown and no lust that is hidden. When we recognize that God gave His life for mankind, despite knowing the very depth of their souls, then we can understand what love really looks like. This is when we can truly understand what it means that God *is* love.

Jesus could have come to earth in all His heavenly glory and demanded obedience and submission. He certainly had the power to do so. Instead, He came and washed man's feet and died a sinner's death to demonstrate genuine love. He knew His death would be our life, and so He loved us unto death.

1 Corinthians 13:1-8 shows that religion without love amounts to nothing in the end. It is the purest form of moral goodness that we can give to another. Every honorable virtue naturally extends from the characteristic of love, as it should since God is love.

"If I speak with the tongues of men and of angels, but do not have love, I have become a noisy gong or a clanging cymbal. If I have the gift of prophecy, and know all mysteries and all knowledge; and if I have all faith, so as to remove mountains, but do not have love, I am nothing. And if I give all my possessions to feed the poor, and if I surrender my body to be burned, but do not have love, it profits me nothing. Love is patient, love is kind and is not jealous; love does not brag and is not arrogant, does not act unbecomingly; it does not seek its own, is not provoked, does not take into account a wrong suffered, does not rejoice in unrighteousness, but rejoices with the truth; bears all things, believes all things, hopes all things, endures all things.

Love never fails"[92]

---

92   1 Corinthians 13:1-8 (NASB)

PART 2:

THE VERDICT

WHO'S ON TRIAL?

"Can a mortal be more righteous than God? Can a man be more pure than his Maker?"[93]

"Is God willing to prevent evil, but not able? Then he is not omnipotent. Is he able, but not willing? Then he is malevolent. Is he both able and willing? Then whence cometh evil? Is he neither able nor willing? Then why call him God?"

Epicurus

---

93   Job 4:17 (NKJV)

Epicurus's statement is an accusation that attacks the power, character, quality, and deity of God. In it, the sole responsibility for man's actions falls on God alone, followed with harsh judgement when God fails to act in accordance with man's way of doing things. Man cleverly is left without a need to take responsibility for his decisions or recognize culpability for his wrongs. It assumes that because God does not do things as man would, or in man's timing, that His position as God is invalidated. Even more specifically, it postulates that God does not exist.

Epicurus's statement is proud and naïve, and it does not account for God's patience and mercy. He wrongly assumed that a lack of immediate action against evil is the same as having an indifferent attitude toward it or being powerless against it. While he was an ancient Greek philosopher, his thoughts are not foreign to modern man. Man believes that God is unaware, unaffected, weak, or does not exist. As a result, he continues in his sin and disobedience. Ecclesiastes 8:11 says, *"Because the sentence against an evil deed is not executed quickly, therefore the hearts of the sons of men among them are given fully to do evil."* This is why God's patience towards man's sin is a reflection of His mercy; it is given while man is overflowing with rebellion.

Those who believe that God should immediately judge and remove all evil do not understand what they are asking for. If God did so, He would bring the same swift judgment on them personally. Evil exists and is active in men's hearts to differing degrees. Due to the presence of evil within us, to remove all evil is to remove all man. Every single man, woman, and child would need to be instantly removed upon their first willful act of evil. God's mercy and patience withhold His immediate hand of judgement until a later time. In doing so, He gives man the opportunity to find forgiveness through Jesus Christ. As the Bible says

"Say to them, 'As I live!' declares the Lord God, 'I take no pleasure in the death of the wicked, but rather that the wicked turn from his way and live. Turn back, turn back from your evil ways! Why then will you die, O house of Israel?"[94]

"The Lord is not slow about His promise, as some count slowness, but is patient toward you, not wishing for any to perish but for all to come to repentance."[95]

While God could in fact remove all evil immediately, His mercy and love for man stop Him from doing so. This temperance is only for a small portion of man's time on earth. At man's death, mercy is exhausted, and judgment comes swiftly. Epicurus's accusation toward God is settled in death, because God does in fact abolish evil. However, in the present, God instead chooses to redeem evil and heal what its power has broken. This act in and of itself is a conquering of evil, because it destroys the present hold that evil has on man. Redemption stops the enslavement and removes the binding of sin. This is something that man has no power to do himself.

Additionally, God is the active restrainer of evil. Without His binding power and the existence of the Holy Spirit upon the earth, the poison of evil would be without limit. God does not neglect evil. He protects us from its full destruction and ruin. There is no moment

94   Ezekiel 33:11 (NASB)
95   2 Peter 3:9 (NASB)

where God's hand is not holding back the full ruin that evil can cause.

The better question is not, "Why hasn't God removed all evil?" but rather, "Why did God permit man to have the ability to choose evil in the first place?"

CHOICE

Choice shows the true nature of man's heart and reveals what is really inside the soul. It allows for decisions to be made outside of compulsion or fear. In terms of morality, the choice for good automatically assumes that there is a choice for evil. They are both inherent in choice.

Genuine relationship and companionship abide in the realm of choice. Choice is a fundamental component of love. One cannot force anyone to love them, they can only force submission and compliance. Even acceptance can eventually be won by force, as is seen in abusive relationships, but love is based on a person's free choice and will. It is an independent decision of the mind in concert with the heart, which unites people in a relationship.

A good relationship has abiding and fundamental characteristics: loyalty, mutual respect and admiration, faithfulness, trust, sacrifice, kindness, authenticity, love, affection, and honesty. If someone in a relationship violates any of those principles, they will most likely destroy it. In that circumstance, that person has fractured something meant to be sacred. We freely give our hearts and minds, and entrust them to someone else, in expectation that they will handle them as a sacred thing. When they do not, our soul feels violated. Trust is so hard to recover once it is lost because the soul of a person was harmed.

The understanding of what is sacred is even greater for intimate and familial relationships. Even the most extreme sinner will give their own life for those they love. This is the uniqueness of the bond that we form with the people who are most dear to us.

In the Bible, there is reference after reference to an intimate, love relationship between God and man. This relationship holds all the same principles and expectations of earthly ones, with the addition of one important component: God entered into this relationship with man while we were in rebellion to Him and while we rejected Him. He entered it without the considerations or qualities that define ours: merit and warrant. He also entered without limiting how far He would go for man. God did not limit the principles of love or self-sacrifice, even to the point of dying for us. This is the fundamental meaning behind Romans 5:6-8:

"Christ died for the ungodly. For scarcely for a righteous man will one die; yet perhaps for a good man someone would even dare to die. But God demonstrates His own love toward us, in that while we were still sinners, Christ died for us."

Because God created man with the intent of genuine relationship and fellowship with Him, the component of freedom had to be included, as a real relationship is inherently free. Additionally, the relationship that He describes in Scripture is familial and intimate, not a blasé acquaintance. It is genuine in all aspects. If God allowed us to be creatures without choice and without knowledge of that understanding, He would have known. I believe that had He made any other decision, it would have meant going against His nature of truth and His character of love. While we would never have known this, God always would. Our love to Him would be fraudulent.

Truth is a fundamental part of God's character. To love is a free decision. God knows more than anyone that love is free. It is behind the nature of the cross. Jesus chose to die freely, as an act of love for man and an act of obedience out of His love for the Father. It is what makes redemption so beautiful. Jesus chose to die, despite every reason not to.

We on the other hand need to have our love restored. Man violates the principles of love, most specifically in our relationship with God. However, we also fail to love our fellow man well. Our understanding of love is shaped by sin. It is based on things that benefit and please us, and it is removed just as easily when those elements change. God, however, understands love in a perfect way. He recognizes that love can be hard, sacrificial, one-sided, and rejected. As such, God loves man in a perfect way in an act of sacrifice and rescue. Jesus' love for mankind was raw, pure, and true. He holds nothing back in his affection for us.

ONLY TWO OPTIONS

Only two viable options exist concerning the cause of all that is wrong in this world: 1) man is the cause, or 2) God is the cause. These options need to be considered when we think about God and the presence of evil. To answer who is truly at fault, we need to assume the validity of both natures being good and see how they fare. Either God is good or man is good.

RULING OUT THE CONTENDERS

First, we need to rule out the contenders to this question: both God and man are good; both God and man are bad; and both God and man are good and bad. If God and man were both good, there would be no presence of evil and sin in the world. "To be" is to deal with the nature of. When one says man is good, they are speaking of his nature "to be", not that he does good or that he has good, but that he *is* good. Most people confuse the fact that man can do good, which is the extension of God's image within us, with man's *being* good. They are not the same.

To be good would be a state of goodness. In that state, there could be no evil or by necessity, it would not be good. When you consider what the world looks like, it is impossible that both man and God are good by nature. If this were so, there would be no existence of evil in the relationship from man to man or from man to God. This is not an accurate view of the world. So the fact that the world contains evil rules out this possibility.

If both God and man were both evil by nature, there would be no presence of good anywhere in the world. Evil cannot bring forth what is good, because its very nature is in opposition to it. It cannot bring forth what it does not have within itself. If evil had good, then by nature it would not be evil. We know this is not an option, because we can clearly see the presence of good throughout our world. The presence of good rules out this possibility.

Lastly, we have to consider if God and man can be both good and bad simultaneously. Let us revisit the nature of good and the nature of evil as a state of being. One cannot "be" good and at the same time "be" bad. This would violate the law of noncontradiction. You cannot "be" one thing and at the same time and in the same sense "be" a different thing. For example, one cannot be both A and not A. That is an impossibility. So, we are left with our first two options to consider: the nature of God, and the nature of man.

WHO THEN IS GOOD?

If man were good and God were bad, there would be no definable presence of good on the earth. Beauty is a definable presence of good, as is warmth and love. These exist universally in our world. Additionally, the presence of good within us, by necessity, must have come from somewhere. If we were created by a god with an evil nature, we would not have the possibility of good. One cannot create with something that they do not possess the quality of. An evil god would have no desire, need, or knowledge to create good, because good would be outside its nature. Additionally, man could not evolve this quality, because we were created without its possibility within us. So, if God were evil by nature, man could never be good or do good on his own.

If man were evil and God were good, there would be a definable presence of good and evil on this earth. We would see man acting in accordance with his nature and a world where corruption extends even to nature, which is what we see. Additionally, while man would not *be* good, he could *do* good, because good is an extension of the nature of

God. It would be present, observable, and distinct on the earth, which also is what we see.

If we concede that God is good and man is evil, then man finds himself as the guilty party. This is uncomfortable but not illogical or without evidence.

ONLY ONE OPTION

We are still left with the existence of permissible evil. This is a dilemma for some people. However, if we accept as truth that God is good, then we must consider permissible evil based on this truth. Its existence assumes that there is a purpose for its being allowed, and the end of its purpose is good. St. Augustine said, "God judged it better to bring good out of evil than to suffer no evil to exist." If the purpose for evil being temporarily allowed is to spare mankind from an immediate judgement, so that he might find forgiveness, then it would be wrong to remove that evil. In doing so, an immediate, eternal judgement without the possibility or hope of redemption would be the tradeoff. If so, the only hope that we have, as sinners, is the world as it is.

There is the understanding that not everyone will be forgiven, but the opportunity must be allowed universally to ensure everyone has the chance. While many will not, it is allowed for those who will.

Furthermore, the faith and love that come from redemption are far more beautiful and genuine than a life without it. I believe this is Augustine's point: redemption is the better thing. He assumes that in God's wisdom, where He knows the end of both possibilities, evil is more beautiful and brings about a greater quality of love and worship than a life without it. This is the wisdom of God.

"If by the Author of Sin, be meant the Sinner, the Agent, or Actor of Sin, or the Doer of a wicked thing; so it would be a reproach and blasphemy, to suppose God to be the Author of Sin. In this sense, I utterly deny God to be the Author of Sin... if, by the Author of Sin, is meant the permitter, or not a hinderer of Sin; and, at the same lime, a disposer of the state of events, in such a manner, for wise, holy, and most excellent ends and purposes, that Sin, if it be permitted or not hindered, will most certainly and infallibly follow: I say, if this be all that is meant, by being the Author of Sin, I do not deny that God is the Author of Sin, (though I dislike and reject the phrase, as that which by use and custom is apt to carry another sense,) it is no reproach for the Most High to be thus the Author of Sin. This is not to be the Actor of Sin, but, on the contrary, of holiness. What God doth herein, is holy; and a glorious exercise of the infinite excellency of his nature."

Jonathan Edwards

LET'S TALK ABOUT JUSTICE

"It is sometimes said, "Justice requires God to do this," referring to some act we know He will perform. This is an error of thinking as well as of speaking, for it postulates a principle of justice outside of God that compels Him to act in a certain way. Of course there is no such principle. If there were it would be superior to God, for only a superior power can compel obedience. The truth is that there is not and can never be anything outside of the nature of God that can move Him in the least degree. All God's reasons come from within His uncreated being. Nothing has entered the being of God from eternity, nothing has been removed, and nothing has been changed.

Justice, when used of God, is a name we give to the way God is, nothing more; and when God acts justly, He is not doing so to conform to an independent criterion, but simply acting like Himself in a given situation. As gold is an element in itself and can never change nor compromise but is gold wherever it is found, so God is God, always, only, fully God, and can never be other than He is. Everything in the universe is good to the degree it conforms to the nature of God and evil as it fails to do so. God is His own self-existent principle of moral equity, and when He sentences evil men or rewards the righteous, He simply acts like Himself from within, uninfluenced by anything that is not Himself."

A.W. Tozer

HOW SHALL GOD JUDGE THE WORLD?

Romans 3:5-6 says *"But if our unrighteousness commend the righteousness of God, what shall we say? Is God unrighteous who taketh vengeance? (I speak as a man) God forbid: for then how shall God judge the world?"* How else will God judge the world? These are the questions that we must wrestle with as people.

Would it be just to have no punishment for the crime that we commit on this earth? Instead of justice, should God allow free entrance into heaven or remove guilty men completely from existence, ensuring that they never pay for what they have done?

If a man kidnaps and rapes a woman, enslaves her for 20 years, and then commits suicide, would it be fair to escape his crime? Is it justice when a guilty man can hire a good lawyer to escape the wrong caused? Is it justice when someone slanders another's name causing them to get fired? Or if someone spreads lies about someone else causing them emotional pain, and getting away with it? Would it be justice if someone stole a car or if they hurt a child and they get no more than a few days in prison? If that was your child, your soul would cry out for justice.

Justice is ingrained in men. As human beings, we are upset when we see injustice. We are angry when we hear about another judge who allowed a crime to go unpunished, an unfaithful politician who took advantage of his position, a "dirty" cop who violated the law, a lawyer who represented the bad guys, and a criminal who got off because he had the money to afford a lawyer who knew his way around the system. Every day, we see the effects of compromise, injustice, and sin, and it angers us. We desire justice to be given for crimes that are committed.

God is no different.

Let us change the focus. What if you are the guilty person? Should it change the requirement just because you are the guilty party? Job 34:33 asks, "Should He (God) repay it according to your terms?"[96] Would that be justice? Man's desire for justice changes when he is on the receiving end of punishment for his crime. For man, there is only room for God's justice when it is falling on someone else or when man agrees that it is warranted. Hitler would be a good example. In that case, God's judgement is acceptable. Man is perfectly fine with the idea that Hitler is in hell. However, the idea that we may have the same destination as Hitler makes us quite uncomfortable. We see ourselves as morally superior to Hitler. We believe our sins are not on the same level as his, so we reject the idea of a similar judgement. We can recognize that men who have done great acts of evil, deserve judgement for them. We even expect it. We just will not accept that our sinful acts require punishment. As such, we judge God for the idea

96   Job 34:33a (NKJV)

of a personal judgement for our own crimes.

However, would it be just for God to excuse you of the same sin He judges another for? Would it be fair to the person you have wronged? If you are being intellectually fair, you would acknowledge that your sin also requires a fine.

WHAT CANNOT PAY YOUR FINE

Man's crimes before God require a sentence, no different than any human court. In our courts, time is measurable and, by design, changes. Our sentencing exists within the expanse of the creation of time. However, when we step into eternity, our sentence is no longer measurable. It exists in the eternal and as such is eternal. There is no beginning or end, there just "is." There is no way to quantify time in a timeless realm, and the gift of forgiveness is only offered in the realm of time. So, where we go is fixed. Due to this truth, the care of our soul is of utmost importance. This is why people teach a dangerous falsehood when they say that our punishment is temporary and can be worked off. Purgatory, reincarnation, and other religious ideas like these do not exist. They were invented as a way to ease our personal understanding that we owe a debt for our sin and also as a tool for religious control. However, what they do provide is evidence that we as humans are fully aware that we are sinners and that judgement awaits.

We cannot measure our debt in any way to allow us to remove it from our soul. God considers holiness to extend beyond mere actions to our mind and our heart. Therefore, our sins are innumerable before Him. I certainly could not calculate how many times I have lied in my life, but even more so, I would not be able to calculate how many times my mind and heart sinned—how often I have coveted, or looked with lust, or felt hate and envy. One cannot satisfy a debt that is without measure.

Also, our state before God disqualifies our ability to pay down our fine, because we come to God as a sinner with compounding sins. We ask God to remove our sins before Him, but we come to Him still active in sin. Even if work and effort could remove our debt, as quickly as it was removed, our daily sin would build it back up again. There would always be a debt balance.

Our motives too would disqualify our sin debts' removal, because we are not necessarily sorry for what we have done as much as we do not want to bear the consequences. We are trying to win God's favor, and that act alone is self-serving and does not genuinely extend from a place of godly sorrow. That is the difference between repentance and earthly sorrow. Repentance is a place of mourning and anguish, because we have sinned against God. Earthly sorrow is the concern with the consequences that we face or the guilt and shame they cause us. It is not concerned that our sins grieve God and break His law. The object for our sorrow is essential. With genuine repentance, man is radically moved by the knowledge that he sinned against the Lord. As a result, he turns from a life marked by sin to a life marked by obedience to the Lord.

Lastly, the payment must be fair and fit the crime. Our sins harm and affect others. They extend to an eternal God first and then to finite man. Our debt must satisfy all the harm caused to everyone, including God, over the full course of our life. It cannot be of lesser value than the crimes committed, because it would not be just and fair. Feeding the poor could not satisfy a debt of murder, even if I fed the poor for 20 years. Our payment must be of equal or greater value than the crime. When we wrong God, we wrong an infinite being. He is infinite in both goodness and measure (timelessness). Our wrong is infinite before Him, because He is not bound in time. How can we, as finite human beings, pay off an infinite debt to God? There is no way man can ever pay that.

Hebrews 9:22 says, *"Indeed, under the law almost everything is purified with blood, and without the shedding of blood there is no forgiveness of sins."*[97] The satisfaction of our debt is our own life, because it is the only thing that we possess that is equal to our lifetime of sin. This is why judgement awaits each of us.

DEATH ROW INMATES

Does God send people to hell? The answer is yes. I do not know why people have such a hard time answering this question honestly. He sends people to hell every day; however, they are sent as a condition of their own guilt. This is no different than a judge sentencing a criminal who has earned his punishment. We are people who have earned hell by our own thoughts, words, and deeds. Hell is justice given for a life of sin and rebellion against God and our fellow man. The notion of the sweet, old lady being wrongfully sent to hell is a fallacy. There is no

---

97   Hebrews 9:22 (ESV)

sweet, old lady who has never, even once, sinned against God or man. It is merely conjecture and a way to pacify one's troubled conscience.

God also sends people who willingly reject Him to hell. These are people who, by choice, have chosen to reject God personally and refuse His forgiveness specifically. This is a different type of rejection, because there is an awareness of the truth of the claims of the Gospel. God merely gives these people what they desire: eternal separation from Him. Furthermore, they have the debt of their sin before them, so they are guilty based on the law as well. Even as you read this, you are either rejecting or embracing what has been written. In the end, it will stand as a judgement or a blessing on your soul.

One thing for certain is that man is in hell by his own volition. In reality, people who reject God on earth, would not want to spend an eternity worshiping God in heaven. In the *Brothers Karamazov*, Dostoevsky stated that some people in hell "…remain proud and fierce even in hell, in spite of their certain knowledge and contemplation of the absolute truth; there are some fearful ones who have given themselves over to Satan and his proud spirit entirely. For such, hell is voluntary and ever consuming; they are tortured by their own choice. For they have cursed themselves, cursing God and life."[98]

I have found that heaven is one of the greatest revealers of man's heart. Mankind likes the idea of heaven and all the blessings it brings, but God is rarely mentioned or thought of as being there. Man's idea of heaven, quite often, does not include Him as present and sovereign,

---

98   Adler, Mortimer. The Great ideas, A Syntopicon 2, Man to World. William Benton, 1952

despite the fact that heaven is where God lives. It is heaven—yes, eternal life—yes, goodness and rest—yes, God—no!

WHY HELL?

The existence of hell is not the result of a character flaw of God but rather the necessary eternal banishment of evil wherever it is found. For God, in eternity, there is no room for compromise with evil. Additionally, it would bring about an afterlife no different than the broken world in which we currently live. Eternity would be a place where there is no escaping brokenness, wickedness, ruin, evil, sickness, and suffering—forever!

The better question is this: why would man choose to reject forgiveness when it is a gift that is free and available to everyone? An anonymous atheist is quoted as saying, "If your God is real, I'd rather burn in hell for all eternity than worship…Him." Hell is a place that some people would go, rather than be with God for eternity, but that often is because what is believed about hell is far different than what it is actually like. Even in some Christian churches, the pains of hell are minimized by teachings that hell is merely a separation from God. Is that an honest statement or just easier for people to tell others? What consequences does the watering down of this truth have on those we share it with?

HELL IS

The truth about hell is that it is a place of eternal punishment. Jesus spoke more about hell than He spoke about heaven. He pleaded with men to flee from the wrath to come. He did not minimize its penalty to make it more palatable to men. On the contrary, He proclaimed that it was better to cut off parts of your body that cause you to sin against God, than to be cast into hell—"…*into the fire that shall never be quenched.*"[99]

Man must understand certain facts about hell to fully grasp the importance of eternity:

1. Hell is a real place. Because God is real, hell is real. The concept of judgement is not imagined but ingrained.

2. Our senses are active in hell; that is, we will feel it.

3. Hell is eternal.

4. Hell is a place of punishment.

5. Hell has fire.

6. No good thing dwells there. Good exists with God, because it comes forth from God.

7. Hell is spiritual agony.

8. Satan does not rule hell. He is bound there like every other prisoner.

Dostoevsky wrote in the *Brothers Karamazov*, "…I think if there were fire in the material sense, they would be glad for it, for, I imagine, that in material agony, their still greater spiritual agony would be forgotten

---

99   Mark 9:45-46 (NKJV)

for a moment."[100] Hell is not a place you want to end up. In Hell, our spirit is destitute of good and alone. Contrary to popular belief, in hell, there is no partying, no community, no pleasure, no relationship, no sex, no friendship, no rest, and no beauty. Nothing good we love here will be found there. It is a place of darkness, emptiness, and torment. It is not unloving to speak honestly about its truth. Its reality warrants our honesty.

Jesus warned about hell and died to save men from that fate. Many have echoed His warning of the punishment that lies before man in hopes that man may seek forgiveness in Jesus Christ. The evidence of our guilt is established throughout the course of our lives on earth. Every moment of every day, we build our own case against ourselves. The evidence is overwhelming and damning.

GUILTY: OVERWHELMING EVIDENCE

- In a 1991 study, sex researcher, Shere Hite, found that 70 percent of married women have cheated on their partners. A follow-up study conducted in 1993 found that 72 percent of married men have as well.[101]

- Every 40 seconds in the United States, a child becomes missing or is abducted. In 2001, 840,279 people (adults and children) were reported missing to the FBI's National Crime Information Center (NCIC). The FBI estimates that 85-90 percent of those

100 Adler, Mortimer. The Great ideas, A Syntopicon 2, Man to World. William Benton, 1952

101 https://www.washingtonpost.com/opinions/five-myths-about-cheating/2012/02/08/gIQANGdaBR_story.html?utm_term=.e3ed5c206860 Accessed April 2017

(roughly 750,000 people or 2,000 per day) reported missing were children: kidnapping by a relative of the victim or "family kidnapping" (49 percent), kidnapping by an acquaintance of the victim or "acquaintance kidnapping" (27 percent), and kidnapping by a stranger to the victim or "stranger kidnapping" (24 percent).[102]

- A "2002 study by Robert Feldman of the University of Massachusetts found that 60 percent of people lied at least once during a 10-minute conversation and told an average of two to three lies." Feldman said of the study, "People tell a considerable number of lies in everyday conversation. It was a very surprising result. We did not expect lying to be such a common part of daily life."[103]

- In 2013, 5,928 hate crime incidents involving 6,933 offenses were reported by our law enforcement partners to the Bureau's Uniform Crime Reporting (UCR) Program. These hate crime incidents impacted a total of 7,242 victims, who are defined as individuals, businesses, institutions, or society as a whole.[104]

- In 2014 "21 million victims are trapped in modern-day slavery" globally. Of that "14.2 million (68%) were exploited for labor,

102 http://www.parents.com/kids/safety/stranger-safety/child-abduction-facts/ Accessed April 2017

103 https://www.umass.edu/newsoffice/article/umass-amherst-researcher-finds-most-people-lie-everyday-conversation Accessed March 2017

104 https://www.fbi.gov/news/stories/latest-hate-crime-statistics-report-released Accessed September 2017

4.5 million were sexually exploited (22%), and 2.2 million (10%) were exploited in state-imposed forced labor." Sadly, "the number of children under the age of 18 [is] estimated at 5.5 million (26%)."[105]

- In 2014, an estimated 1,564 children died from abuse and neglect in the United States. More than 700,000 children are abused in the U.S. annually. Neglect is the most common form of maltreatment. Of the children who experienced maltreatment or abuse, nearly 80% suffered neglect; 18% suffered physical abuse; and 9% suffered sexual abuse. (Some children are poly-victimized and have suffered more than one form of maltreatment.) Approximately four of five abusers are the victims' parents. A parent of the child victim was the perpetrator in 78% of substantiated cases of child maltreatment.[106]

- In 2015 in the United States, "there were an estimated 1,197,704 violent crimes committed around the nation." Of that number, 15,696 were murders, 90,185 were rapes, and 327,374 were robberies.[107]

- The 2016 Identity Fraud Study, released by Javelin Strategy & Research, found that $15 billion was stolen from 13.1 million U.S. consumers in 2015 compared with $16 billion and 12.7

105 http://www.humanrightsfirst.org/resource/human-trafficking-numbers Accessed September 2017

106 http://www.nationalchildrensalliance.org/wp-content/uploads/2014/04/NCA-Media-Guide.pdf Accessed October 2018

107 https://www.fbi.gov/news/stories/latest-crime-statistics-released Accessed September 2017

million victims a year earlier. In the past 6 years, identity thieves have stolen $112 billion.[108]

- An estimated 160-203 million people have died in wars during the 20th century.

- The estimated number of people who cheat on their taxes each year is 1,625,000.[109]

- The amount stolen annually from U.S. businesses by employees is $50 billion.[110]

- Nineteen people become victims of identity theft every minute.[111]

- Liquor laws that limit the sales of alcohol, such as sales to minors, are broken regularly across all of the states.[112]

- On average, nearly 20 people per minute are physically abused by an intimate partner in the United States. During one year, this equates to more than 10 million women and men. One in three women and one in four men have been victims of physical violence by an intimate partner within their lifetime.[113]

There is no end to these types of statistics. Whether we are talking about hatred, gossip, hypocrisy, jealousy, revenge, pride, adultery, theft,

108 http://www.iii.org/fact-statistic/identity-theft-and-cybercrime Accessed September 2017

109 http://www.statisticbrain.com/how-many-people-cheat-on-taxes/ Accessed September 2017

110 http://www.statisticbrain.com/employee-theft-statistics/ Accessed September 2017

111 https://www.safesmartliving.com/identity-theft-statistics/ Accessed September 2017

112 http://www.schatzanderson.com/information-and-resources/20-common-felony-crimes-u-s/

113 http://ncadv.org/learn-more/statistics Accessed September 2017

lying, cheating, idolatry, violence, pornography, etc., the statistics do not lie. Average people—not dictators, serial killers, and mass murders—commit sinful acts every single day. We sin against God and each other, and in many ways, we enjoy it. As Mortimer Adler points out, "Sin is itself enjoyed for its own sake, and the disobedient act is pleasant because it is forbidden."[114] Augustine reflected on sin in his confessions. In discussing his enjoyment on stealing pears in his youth, he said, "Once I had gathered them, I threw them away, tasting only my sin and savouring that with delight; for if I took so much as a bite of any one of those pears, it was the sin that sweetened it."[115]

We will and do hurt the people we love for our own selfishness and the pursuit of happiness. We will lie and cheat if it suits our needs, including when we understand we are doing so at the expense of someone innocent or someone we love. Regardless of evidence, reason, or truth, man will not believe in any god that prevents him from having his own way. We believe in a god that suits our lusts and allows us to live however we want, without punishment. The god we accept is as human, sinful, and deceptive as we are. Romans 1 speaks about how man, *"... changed the glory of the incorruptible God into an image made like corruptible man—and birds and four-footed animals and creeping things."*[116] And man *"exchanged the truth of God for the lie, and worshiped and served the creature rather than the Creator, who is blessed forever. Amen."*[117]

If God challenges our lifestyle, religious upbringing, political views, accepted moral compass, financial pursuits, desires, or anything that

---

114   Adler, Mortimer. The Great ideas, A Syntopicon 2, Man to World. William Benton, 1952
115   Adler, Mortimer. The Great ideas, A Syntopicon 2, Man to World. William Benton, 1952
116   Romans 1:23 (NKJV)
117   Romans 1:25 (NKJV)

we want to do in this world, we reject Him, plain and simple. When we are finally faced with the true God and see His holiness and hear of His justice, we accuse Him of being wrong for judging the sin and rebellion we love. We get angry at Him for permitting evil and get angry at Him when He judges it. Despite all we do, somehow God is always left responsible:

1. God in His mercy and patience for a time permits evil; therefore, He is wrong.

2. God judges evil; therefore, He is wrong.

3. God allows choice, and man chooses sin; therefore, God is wrong.

4. God shows the pathway home and man does not believe and is lost; therefore, God is wrong.

5. God sends messengers and man rejects them; therefore, God is wrong.

6. God provides the Bible, and man rejects it; therefore, God is wrong.

7. God sends His Son to pay for our sins, and man rejects His son and faces judgement; therefore, God is wrong.

8. God comes to earth to free man, and man chooses sin; therefore, God is wrong.

9. God is crucified for man, by man; therefore, God is wrong.

10. God warns man that his choices have consequences, and man falls into those consequences; therefore, God is wrong.

11. Man hates death. God provides life. Man rejects life. Therefore, God is wrong.

The truth is, we do not want to face any consequences for the lives that we live. We want to do what we want and pass into heaven and live in peace. A god who allows this is the god that we want and believe in. However, if God allowed this, heaven indeed would be hell, and the next life would look no better than it does now. Whether we like it or not, hell is warranted, so God is vindicated.

Is there justice for the evil done in this world? There is indeed a perfect justice and a time for every man to give an account of His life before God. *As 1 Samuel 20:3 says, "but truly as the LORD liveth, and as thy soul liveth, there is but a step between me and death."* Hell is before every man, but so is hope in Jesus.

"Consider that all these torments of body and soul are without intermission. Be their suffering ever so extreme, be their pain ever so intense, there is no possibility of their fainting away, no, not for one moment… They are all eye, all ear, all sense. Every instant of their duration it may be said of their whole frame that they are 'Trembling alive all o'er, and smart and agonize at every pore.' And of this duration there is no end… Neither the pain of the body nor of soul is any nearer an end than it was millions of ages ago."

John Wesley, Sermon 73[118]

"Who knowing the judgment of God, that they which commit such things are worthy of death, not only do the same, but have pleasure in them that do them."[119]

---

118   http://wesley.nnu.edu/john-wesley/the-sermons-of-john-wesley-1872-edition/sermon-73-of-hell/ - Accessed September 2018

119   Romans 1:32 (KJV)

JESUS: SAVIOR AND KING

"Truly, truly, I say to you, before Abraham was born, I am."[120]

"You will never know the fullness of Christ until you know the emptiness of everything but Christ"

Charles Spurgeon

---

120   John 8:58 (NASB)

The modern view of Jesus is often idolatry, not because Jesus is not God, but because man's view of Jesus often is not biblically accurate. There are differing views about Jesus in this culture. Some people act as though Jesus is some weak beggar in need of us…pathetic and crying out to mankind, hoping for someone to respond to Him. They see Him as their equal, their homeboy, a "good" man or teacher, but not God. He is someone that they can dismiss completely if they so choose.

Churches can fall into this idolatry. Too often, they try to fit Jesus into the mass of other cultural icons, as if He is just another interesting person or another person of significance. However, there is no comparison for Jesus. Ray Comfort put it so well, *"Comparing Jesus with history's greatest of human leaders is like comparing the sun to a flashlight with no batteries."*[121]

Churches try to make Jesus relevant to the culture, as if His relevance is questionable. The definition of relevant is, *"bearing upon or connected with the matter in hand; pertinent."*[122] When it comes to mankind, there is no one more relevant than Jesus. If the matter at hand is humanity, then we do not need to make Jesus relevant; He already is.

In order to reach the culture, churches are unknowingly undermining the very thing that makes Jesus relevant: that He is man's God and King. Jesus is the answer to the judgement, evil, and ruin that encompasses this universe. We err when we bring Him down to our

---

121   https://www.facebook.com/official.Ray.Comfort/posts/535364659817345
      Accessed November 2018

122   https://www.dictionary.com/browse/relevant?s=t Accessed 29 September 2018

level or compare Him to others. There is no room for that with Jesus. Making Jesus relatable may bring sinners into church, but it will not bring them to their knees in worship and faith. It will not save them, because it undermines the authority and necessity of Jesus as God. It offers a false and impotent vision of who Jesus is and why He came. The glory of the gospel is that God Himself bore the punishment that we deserved to free us from the wrath to come, not that God became man to give us our best life now.

GOD BECAME MAN

God became man in the person of Jesus Christ, entering the world that He created and governed. His entrance into time ripped the veil of darkness, exposing light to a lost and hopeless people. The birth of Jesus unseated the power of Satan and the hold that sin had on mankind. Jesus is the infinite God who stepped into His finite creation to fulfill the law we could not fulfill and to conquer evil, sin, and death for us.

Jesus says of Himself:

1. "I am the resurrection and the life. Whoever believes in me, though he die, yet shall he live."[123]

2. "I and the Father are one."[124]

3. "Most assuredly, I say to you, before Abraham was, I AM."[125]

4. "I am the way, and the truth, and the life. No one comes to the

---

123   John 11:25 (ESV)
124   John 10:30 (ESV)
125   John 8:58 (NKJV)

Father except through me."[126]

5. "Whoever believes in the Son has eternal life; whoever does not obey the Son shall not see life, but the wrath of God remains on him."[127]

6. "I told you that you would die in your sins, for unless you believe that I am he you will die in your sins."[128]

7. "I am the true vine, and My Father is the vinedresser."[129]

8. "Believe me that I am in the Father and the Father is in me."[130]

Jesus is called:

1. "Alpha and Omega, the beginning and the end, the first and the last."[131]

2. "King of Kings and Lord of Lords."[132]

3. "The great I Am."[133]

4. "God and Savior."[134]

5. "Lord and Savior."[135]

6. "…God over all…"[136]

---

126   John 14:6 (ESV)

127   John 3:36 (ESV)

128   John 8:24 (ESV)

129   John 15:1 (ESV)

130   John 14:11 (ESV)

131   Rev 22:13 (NKJV)

132   Rev 19:16 (NASB)

133   John 8:58 (NASB)

134   2 Peter 1:1 (ESV), Titus 2:13 (ESV)

135   2 Peter 1:11, 2:20, 3:18 (ESV)

136   Romans 9:5 (ESV)

If a vision of Jesus exists in your mind that is limited or weak, one of a mere person whom you can dismiss, then you have the wrong Jesus. There is no dismissing the real Jesus, not in this world or the next. The biblical Jesus does not ever present that as an option. He does not present Himself as one amongst many, either. There is only one vision that Jesus permits of Himself, and that is of man's sole God and Savior.

SENTENCED TO DEATH

The assumption that God is weak or indifferent toward evil is a failure to understand the purpose of the cross and the power of the One who hung on it. Jesus is the very answer to all the "Why does God allow evil?" questions. The cross demonstrated to man that God is not indifferent or unaware of sin. On the contrary, His death was a warning to all that sin—and that God—will judge man according to His works.

The death of Jesus was one of suffering and pain in the body and spirit. He bore God's wrath; He endured man's violence; He took on man's sin, bearing in His flesh and spirit what holiness had never touched; He experienced abandonment, reproach, loneliness, and humiliation, and He sustained physical weakness and temptation and went through bodily death. Jesus also endured a divine separation from God the Father. It was a loss that we will never be able to understand, even if we lived for all eternity.

The death of Jesus had to pay our debt in full. It had to satisfy the law completely so that man could go free. It was not less than the full measure of debt we owed. It paid every last part in quality, satisfaction, and degree of worth. Every drop of His blood had a purpose; every moment He hung paid a tremendous fine. Jesus suffered an eternity's worth of wrath, bearing the full penalty of sin, in the span of a few hours. I cannot imagine what that must have been like, but I know that without it, mankind would have no hope.

IT IS FINISHED

On the cross, Jesus brought evil to its knees, destroying its power and eternal penalties. His sacrificial act went beyond preventing evil— it laid waste to it completely. His life, death, and resurrection answers the accusation of every accuser of God. With a powerful act of victory, He said, "It is finished," and it was done. This is the relevance of Jesus. He crushed the devil and rendered him impotent: *"... The Son of God appeared for this purpose, to destroy the works of the devil."*[137] He alone is man's Savior! Jesus is the answer to evil.

My cousin, Pastor Dave Figueroa, preached a sermon about the trial of Jesus before His crucifixion. He discussed how in movies Jesus is portrayed as some weak God under the power and judgement of man. He explained how and why that image is truly unbiblical and used an illustration that showed a more appropriate image of Jesus at His trial. Specifically, he used the picture of Superman bound with handcuffs before his human captives. Anyone looking at the picture would clearly see that Superman was not being held captive by the

---

137   1 John 3:8 (NASB)

power of the guards surrounding him.

The illustration of Superman was not a reference to the physical stature or physical appearance of Jesus. It was an illustration of the power behind the One who was bound. It was a power that Jesus Himself chose to lay down to people who foolishly presumed they were in control of what happened to Him. It was Jesus, not the bonds or the guards, who kept Himself restrained. At any moment, if He had chosen, He could free Himself from those bonds. *He* chose to be in subjection to man, not the other way around. As my cousin pointed out, it was man, not Jesus, under trial that day. Never was Jesus on trial *by* man; Jesus was on trial *for* man, and that is a big difference.

People do not disregard the truths about Jesus merely because they are hard to believe, or they find them impossible. I do not believe that the impossibility bothers people at all. It is the *possibility* that frightens them. They disregard these truths because of the fear and smallness it brings up in us. The knowledge that all will one day face a God who is powerful enough to create the universe, and yet understands what it is like to be human, is frightening. It leaves man without excuses to hide behind. Man is unable to claim that He does not understand them, because He lived as one of them and identifies with their humanity. A God who can enter His own creation, whose words caused all that is seen and unseen, is beyond any of men's ability to defend themselves against. It causes mankind to recognize how small, defenseless, and truly exposed they are.

I believe that much unbelief is fueled by fear and not lack of evidence. It is far easier to calm the conscience by believing in a god that we can fool and outsmart, or to accept that God does not exist, than to believe in a God as powerful as Jesus Christ.

JESUS IS

RISEN!

If there were anything that would have invalidated the claims of Jesus' being God and stopped Christianity in its tracks, it would have been a closed tomb filled with an unrisen Jesus. This is simply not the case. As John Dominic Crossan put it, "That he was crucified is as sure as anything historical can ever be."[138] The resurrection of Jesus Christ is the greatest historical event of all time! This one event had a lasting global impact that is still felt today.

Many books go into great detail about the evidence surrounding the resurrection. I am not going to make the case, because it has already been done so well by others. However, I will note that if ever there were a time to discredit the claim of the resurrection, it would have been in the time of the early church for two reasons:

1. While it is true that men, being deceived, die in support of falsehood, men do not die to support something they know is a lie, especially if the death would be a terrible one, as believed was the case with most of the disciples. Many of the men who walked with Jesus died for Him and the fact of the resurrection. They also suffered physical torture and torment for the truth of the resurrected Jesus. The early church would have fallen apart under the lie of the resurrection,

---

138 Jesus: A Revolutionary Biography, p. 145

but these men knew that Jesus rose bodily from the dead and were willing to die, because they knew it was true. They personally witnessed the resurrected Jesus and that fact gave them courage to face death.

2. The people outside the early church would have been the first to dispute the claims of the resurrection. It is interesting to note that while we do have non-biblical accounts of the resurrection, there are no accounts that contradict the resurrection of Jesus Christ. This is relevant, because many people in that age would have gladly disputed the claim, unless of course there was nothing to dispute.

Think about the significance of this in modern times. Imagine if Donald Trump died and certain members of the Republican party falsely claimed that he rose from the dead. Do you really believe the news agencies would not write to correct and dispute these claims? Jesus Christ was the central topic in that time, as we see from the response of the two disciples to Jesus on the road to Emmaus: "Then the one whose name was Cleopas answered and said to Him, 'Are You the only stranger in Jerusalem, and have You not known the things which happened there in these days?'"[139] If the resurrection of Jesus had been a lie, it would have been disputed by people aware of it, especially because the resurrection of Jesus challenged the authority of the Romans and Jews.

The resurrection of Jesus Christ was the death blow to Satan, evil and death, and the moment where every prisoner was set free. It was a point in time where hope was actualized for everyone. This is the relevance of Jesus: freedom!

139   Luke 24:18 (NASB)

BEAUTIFUL!

Why do people try to change Jesus to fit the culture? The true Jesus is the only one who can reach them. Jesus ate with sinners, healed the sick, comforted the marginalized, exposed and rebuked the hypocrite, challenged the wayward, sought out those who felt guilt and shame, gave merit to women and children, saw value in the lame and handicapped, confronted the cynic and doubter, cared for the poor, had compassion on the prodigal, freed those under bondage and oppression, gave sight to the blind, stood in front of prostitutes, touched the lepers, gave purpose to the marginalized, forgave the sinner, sought the lost, loved the loveless, pointed man to the Father, confronted the "good," calmed the storm, fed the hungry, and wept with the broken. If those people do not comprise a perfect picture of this world and our culture, then none exists. He met everyone right where they were and knew their particular needs. He gave fully and totally of Himself, even to the end. In the last moments before His death, He was still interceding and pleading for His enemies, saying, "Father, forgive them, for they know not what they do."[140]

This is the God who created the world in which we live and gave man the breath we breathe. Jesus designed, ordered, and spoke the universe into being by His knowledge, wisdom, and power. He brought forth time, energy, space, and matter. Jesus defeated evil and its power, conquered death by His resurrection, and freed man both eternally and personally. He is the Lion of Judah and the great I AM. Jesus is God, Lord, Savior, and King. There is no place for others amongst Him. There is no one but Jesus.

---

140   Luke 23:24 (ESV)

Jesus is everything, or there is nothing!

"When you think of it, really there are four fundamental questions of life. You've asked them, I've asked them, every thinking person asks them. They boil down to this: origin, meaning, morality and destiny. How did I come into being? What brings life meaning? How do I know right from wrong? Where am I headed after I die?" When you take the answers of Christ to those four questions, there is no parallel that brings individually, correspondingly true answers to those individual questions. And then you put the four together, there's no other worldview that brings such a coherent set of answers, correspondingly true individually, coherently whole when you put them together. The person of Christ is so unique that no honest seeker can deny it once you have looked at his answers to these questions."[141]

Ravi Zacharias

REDEMPTION:

An Appeal to the Beautiful

N / redemp·tion / Latin redemptio

"Repurchase of…prisoners; the act of procuring the deliverance of persons… from the possession and power of captors by the payment of an equivalent; ransom; release; as the redemption of prisoners taken in war"[142]

---

142 http://webstersdictionary1828.com/Dictionary/redemption Accessed October 2017

DOES GOD EXIST?

Christopher Hitchens once said, "What can be asserted without evidence can also be dismissed without evidence." I love this comment, because so much of atheism exists in the possible not the factual. This comment is as much a deathblow to their ideology as they imagine that it is to ours. That being said, I have come to believe that it is not a lack of evidence but an unwillingness to accept evidence that hinders people from believing that God exists. The truth is that there is sufficient and reasonable evidence for the existence of God. Anyone who enters into the search for God, with humility and faith, will find that He absolutely exists.

However, God exists beyond our present visual senses and capabilities. This is difficult for those who need to see God to believe. There is proof of His existence all around us for anyone willing to consider the evidence. More specifically, there is proof not merely that God exists but that Jesus is God. Nevertheless, there is an aspect of humility that must come first before we can know the truth. There is also an aspect of faith—not saving faith, but believing faith. Hebrews 11:6 says, *"...for he who comes to God must believe that He is, and that He is a rewarder of those who diligently seek Him."*[143] Man must be willing to consider the possibility of God and, by doing so, be humble enough to accept that man is not the sole ruler, designer, or final authority of his life. First, a few questions must be dealt with before one can fairly examine the existence of God. Someone would need to ask themselves:

---

143   Hebrews 11:6 (NKJV)

1. Is there any evidence that would be enough for me to believe God exists? If so, what would it be?

2. What evidence would at least cause me to consider the existence of God?

3. Do I even have that possibility open?

4. Am I looking to approach this topic honestly and with an open mind, or am I merely looking to discredit and call into question the evidence of God?

One of the strongest forces to overcome is the decision of the human mind. If a person's mind is made up and unwilling to open to another idea, there is no amount of evidence that will ever convince them otherwise, because they are unwilling. They have already determined in their mind that God does not exist, and that is an impossible supposition to overcome without a personal consent of the mind. Such a mind is determined and much like a vault without a key. As we see by atheist Martin Rowson's statement, *"If God proved he existed, I still wouldn't believe in him.... I don't believe in God, not because I can't but because I don't want to.*"[144]

When someone has already ruled out the existence of God, any evidence they are shown will either be rejected, doubted, mocked, minimized, or dismissed. If I show someone reasonable proof of the miraculous and they dismiss it because they feel it's fantastical, it is not a lack of evidence but rather the person's refusal to accept the evidence.

144   https://www.spectator.co.uk/2008/03/if-god-proved-he-existed-i-still-wouldnt-believe-in-him/ Accessed 20 October 2018

If I demonstrate the probability of God through logical arguments and sound reason, and someone ignores or disregards the logic, then that is an issue with acceptance rather than reason. If I point to fulfilled prophecies and historical and scientific evidence, and I am met with cynicism to factual examples, then the problem is not with the evidence. If I mention that Jesus is known to be a good man globally, yet He himself claimed to be more than a man—in fact claimed to be God and if one rejects His claims of divinity yet believes He was a good man, then it is clearly an issue of faith.

Judas walked with Jesus as one of His apostles. Many of the religious leaders watched as Jesus performed countless miracles. Yet they would not enter by faith into His gospel or believe that He was God. One must approach God through faith, because God determined it to be so. There will always be people who refuse every evidence presented to them. It is not that the evidence does not exist; it is rejection that fuels unbelief. Martin Rowson pointed out, *"Even a personal appearance by the Almighty wouldn't do the trick."*[145] God acknowledges that such a man exists and calls him foolish; "The fool has said in his heart, *There is* no God."[146]

YOU CANNOT RUN FROM GOD

Religion is considered sacred to most of the world. Even with the spread of evolutionary teaching and humanist thought, mankind has yet to give up the belief that God exists. "More than 9 in 10 Americans

145   https://www.spectator.co.uk/2008/03/if-god-proved-he-existed-i-still-wouldnt-believe-in-him/ Accessed 20 October 2018

146   Psalm 14:1 (NKJV)

still say "yes" when asked the basic question "Do you believe in God?"[147]

"A comprehensive demographic study of more than 230 countries and territories conducted by the A Pew Research Center's Forum on Religion & Public Life estimates that there are 5.8 billion religiously affiliated adults and children around the globe, representing 84% of the 2010 world population of 6.9 billion."[148]

The sheer number of people who believe in God supports the probability of God's existence. Dan Brown said, "Wide acceptance of an idea is not proof of its validity."[149] While this statement is not illogical, it also is not absolute. While it *may* be the case that it is not proof of an idea's validity, it does not negate that it also may be proof of it. It is not victorious in its statement.

God has placed an idea in our souls that leads us to seek Him while He may be found. The belief in God is alive and present, placed deep within the fabric of man. There is no force, theory, or idea that will ever have the power to stop it. There is a mountain of evidence for God's existence.

GOD IS THE ARGUMENT

To even consider the existence of God, one must first begin with a proper view of God and work from there. Any other thought of

147   http://news.gallup.com/poll/147887/Americans-Continue-Believe-God.aspx
        Accessed April 2016

148   https://unitedcor.org/sites/default/files/edit-contentfile/butte_county/Internation-
        al%20-%20Pew%20Religious%20Study.pdf Accessed April 2016

149   https://www.goodreads.com/work/quotes/6600281-the-lost-symbol
        Accessed April 2016

God is, by virtue of definition, not God. The starting point of the Judeo-Christian God is used as a contrast point to undermine, dispel, or challenge Him, yet ironically, it proves His preeminence. In one's desire to overthrow, usurp, or challenge God, they are recognizing His position as the one true God, not just God, but the God of the Bible. Every argument used to dispel Him points to the "Who" it is trying to dispel. It is the subconscious universal truth that our mind naturally moves toward…like gravity.

Let me explain further. Every thought, teaching, or argument about God has a point of claim, a place of origination. When people try to contrast God versus "something" or try to argue that God does not exist, they have to go to this point of claim. They have to indicate the "who" they are referencing. This point of origination is where they build their arguments against God or for their personal understanding of God. They attempt to deconstruct God in favor of their view, by working out from Him, to prove their reasoning. An example would look something like this…The fact that there is evil and suffering in this world proves that God does not exist. This thought has an obvious underlying premise—"If God existed, evil and suffering would not exist." There is a second underlying hidden premise, one that assumes a claim about the nature of God. It automatically assumes that "God is all good and all powerful." This claim is inherent in the question, "If God existed, evil and suffering wouldn't exist." The character traits "all good" and "all powerful", in relation to God, should be evidenced by a correction or removal of evil. According to this line of reasoning, because this is not true, God does not exist. The statement is really this—"God is all powerful and all good, and evil and suffering exist. Either God is not all powerful and/or all good, and therefore not God, or God does not in fact exist."

My argument does not deal with the fallacy of this statement but rather the fact of its existence. The character principle, all powerful and all good, is almost a universal understanding of God. One starts there to disprove it. This is true of any argument against God. To disprove Him, one must begin with Him, and many times, one must also end with Him. He is the argument. Even in disproving Him, one acknowledges His existence.

One cannot run from the thought of God. The fact of His existence is deeply understood in our minds. We understand truths and characteristics about God even when we deny that He is real. There is no escaping Him. As a result, unbelief is essentially a rebellion against reason and inherent truth. It is why God says, "...*men, who suppress the truth in unrighteousness, because what may be known of God is manifest in them, for God has shown it to them. For since the creation of the world His invisible attributes are clearly seen, being understood by the things that are made, even His eternal power and Godhead, so that they are without excuse, because, although they knew God, they did not glorify Him as God, nor were thankful, but became futile in their thoughts, and their foolish hearts were darkened. Professing to be wise, they became fools.*"[150]

Unbelief can be fueled by hypocrisy found in religion, hurt experienced in a church environment, wars and abuse in the name of God, confusion at the amount of god possibilities, cultural fears and

150   Romans 1:18-22 (NKJV)

influence, arrogance, and rebellion. There are countless reasons why people reject God. There is always a reason that one can find to reject God if they really want to.

That being said, there is one evidence that is so powerful and difficult to refute that it is the one place skeptics do not like to go— evidence of the redeemed heart. This powerful conversion happens when a person turns from one way of living and, by faith in the Gospel, experiences a dramatic transformation. Additionally, it is evidence that is within one's ability to check and confirm in the present time.

BORN AGAIN – EVIDENCE OF GOD

I believe everyone knows or will meet one person in their lifetime who radically changes course. I am not talking about stopping bad habits and behaviors, cleaning up foul language, or temporary, common change. I am talking about a complete transformation of life. A radical shift that is peculiar, identifiable, and remarkable.

It is possibly the person you know who "found religion" and yet is unlike others who just "do church." Maybe you met them afterwards, but you recognize they are different. It could be that they are unique in their views and guided by different principles and morals than cultural norms. It could be the person who quietly leaves a conversation the minute it veers into inappropriate topics. Whatever the case is, someone personally knows that they were once very different from who they are now.

What is significant about this experience is that this change is observable by others. It is first-hand proof, witnessed and verified by others, of a change that can only be attributed to a movement of God in the life of the individual. There will be no need for them to tell anyone. Others will see it for themselves and speak about it. At times, they may even feel it. Something about the changed person will make others' own souls uneasy or uncomfortable. It will not necessarily be anything purposeful. Their presence alone may cause it. They will be characterized by hope in darkness, faith in trials, steadfastness in persecution, a definite moral rectitude, loyalty to Jesus, a life lived genuinely not perfectly, healing from brokenness, a life of forgiveness and confession of sin, a firm belief in what happens after death, courage, integrity, humility, love, meekness, compassion, surrender, joy, etc.

This is what is called being born again, getting saved, or any other similar statement. This soul rebirth happened to me in 2004. Whether people believe Christians' claims or not, our change is evidence of the existence of God. I have had people minimize my statement of fact when I tell them why I am different, but that is irrelevant to its truth. I know emphatically that I am new.

When I think about the old me, it is as though I am looking at someone I once knew a long time ago. I am that girl, and at the same time, I am not. I *was* her. She died when I was born again.

REDEMPTION

"Redemption—In theology, the purchase of God's favor by the death and sufferings of Christ; the ransom or deliverance of sinners from the bondage of sin and the penalties of God's violated law by the atonement of Christ."[151]

---

151 http://webstersdictionary1828.com/Dictionary/redemption Accessed 6 October 2018

147

To be redeemed is to be freed from enslavement, often through the payment of a ransom. Our sin against God's law requires justice- a debt that we owe and must pay. We were enslaved to the debt and, hence, are under the penalty of the law. Jesus took the debt that we owed and paid it by offering His own life as a ransom in place of ours. The law is satisfied through His sacrifice, and we are legally freed from the penalty that we once owed. His action restored our broken relationship with God. It heals our soul and makes us new. We are no longer far from God, because this act brings us near. This is what happens in the spiritual realm.

In the physical realm, we no longer reject what is holy and no longer desire what is evil and sinful. Our mind, actions, and heart change. Our passions and desires change. Our purpose and our direction changes. Our brokenness and our bondage changes. Redemption is a cataclysmic event within the person where God enters man, redeems him, and renews him to his first nature: good. In that moment and for the rest of eternity, our soul belongs to Jesus and our heart beats after His.

SPIRITUAL BEAUTY

There is a unique and inexpressible beauty to redemption. Those who have been redeemed know the unmistakable change that our souls have experienced from being set free. It is truly impossible to understand what it is like outside of the presence of God's Spirit within a person. There is an awareness of what we have been rescued from and an incredible love for the One who rescued us—Jesus Christ. This understanding both defines and changes us eternally.

Redemption is a story interwoven throughout man's history. It has within it all the great elements of epic tales, as if they were clues pointing in a certain direction. It contains the final war with good overcoming evil, a hero and a villain, sacrifice, love, the triumph of the underdog, betrayal, forgiveness, brotherhood, and death. Yet despite its similarities to epic tales, the greatest beauty is in its differences.

In epic tales, the triumph of the underdog is personally satisfying to us. We watch ordinary, insignificant, or unexpected characters turn into great heroes. Unbeknownst to them, they become people that they were always destined to be. The story usually has as much to do with them figuring out and believing their destiny, as it does with them fulfilling it. The ordinary becoming great appeals to all our hearts, as this is a desire we often have for ourselves.

In the same way, the most significant part of redemption is the identity of the hero but for an entirely different reason. Unlike the story of an ordinary man becoming great, redemption is about a great, glorious, all-powerful God humbly taking on the ordinary. The God of the universe became flesh like one of us.

In those epic stories, sacrifice is made for the good, the worthy, the needy, and the noble. However, in the redemption story, the sacrifice is made for the wicked, the rebellious, the lost, and the enemy of the very King who has come to rescue and save them.

In redemption:

1. Death births life, and the Creator becomes His creation.

2. The King becomes stained while the enemy becomes clean.

3. Hope is realized, and man's soul is healed.

4. Good crushes evil, breaking its power and hold on man.

5. Freedom is won for the slave.

6. The enemy becomes an heir to the very throne he once rebelled against.

Redemption is about the birth of a brotherhood, forged by the Holy Spirit and united by the power of a limitless love. It is about the heart of the enemy healed by the love of the King that he once rejected.

It is the most beautiful story a man has ever heard. But unlike the great fictional epic tales, redemption is true. I should know; it is my story too. I have been overwhelmed by a grace and love that I am incapable of expressing accurately, other than to say that it has changed every part of who I am and healed every wound and pain that once defined and controlled me.

When people say to me that I cannot prove that God exists, they do not realize that I am proof of His existence. This is why I can't join a hypothetical dialogue that assumes that God doesn't exist. I know that God is real, because I have been forever changed by Him, and daily He is with me.

"In Him we have redemption through His blood, the forgiveness of sins, according to the riches of His grace"[152]

"And he said, "He who has ears to hear, let him hear."[153]

---

152   Eph 1:7 (NKJV)
153   Mark 4:9 (ESV)

WHY ARE WE HERE?
TWO PATHS

"Religion was invented when the first con man met the first fool."

Mark Twain

"I love to think of nature as an unlimited broadcasting station, through which God speaks to us every hour, if we will only tune in."

George Washington Carver

"Humans have always wondered about the meaning of life...life has no higher purpose than to perpetuate the survival of DNA...life has no design, no purpose, no evil and no good, nothing but blind pitiless indifference."

Richard Dawkins

HOLDING ONTO NOTHING

When belief in God is removed, mankind spends all his time, money, and efforts trying to answer questions whose answers make no sense outside of God. Why am I here? What is my purpose? These questions assume "a why" designed specifically for them, yet this cannot be without a thinking Being (God) assigning that why. As Richard Dawkins' quote above states, man has no real purpose other than the survival of DNA. Yet despite humanist teachings, man believes that a definite purpose belongs to him.

Indeed, without God, man would be a grand cosmic joke. In our finest and at our best, we would live to 100 plus or minus years old. Our accomplishments would be like dust in the wind, and our memories would be a sad echo in an unintelligible darkness. The height of mankind and all our triumphs would mean nothing. We would be fundamentally unimportant to the universe. There would be no protection from cataclysmic events, no orchestrator or designer over man's lives, no righting of wrongs; nothing! If something happened to this planet, apart from the personal tragedy to the inhabitants of earth, who would care?

For a small period of time, we are given life. In the end, we will die, and our lives will become nonlife. What people thought about us—good or bad—will not matter. What we did in this world—good or bad—will not matter. Whether we loved someone or were loved will not matter. Our children will not matter. Our history will not matter. Our politics will not matter. Our wealth and achievements will not matter. Nothing will matter.

If I were the very worst person who ever lived, eventually everyone who felt that about me would die, so who cares? Once I am dead, I am gone. It would not matter what anyone thought about me, because I would have no conscious awareness.

MORAL OBLIGATION

I have heard arguments that we are obligated to live this life as moral and good people, because this is all there is. Why? Who cares? Why would that matter? You would have zero recollection of the life that you lived and neither would anyone else. As quickly as your life began, your memory would fade until it was no more. Not one thing would matter to you—not one regret, not one wish, not one moment, not one feeling, and not one person. The murderous sex offender and the holiest religious person, regardless of their life would share the same fate—nothingness.

In many ways, humans would be worse off than animals. An animal does not strive for futile things or regard the unnecessary. It lives its raw, animalistic life. What it wants, it takes. It has little or no regard for feelings, emotional hurts, fame, fortune, purpose, past, or future. It lives freely in the now.

The only creatures worse off than humans would be humans who never really "lived": the rule followers, the fearful, the unhappy, the moral, the civil; they would be bigger cosmic jokes, because they never used their one opportunity to live. But then again, who cares? It is not like they would realize this anyway, once they were gone.

And what of the moral condition? Some would argue that morally it makes sense to live in such a way that benefits the earth, the animal kingdom, and humanity's survival. But I ask you again, why? There would be zero reason for us to live morally. We would have zero obligation to anyone and owe no one anything. We would be nothing more than an animal. We would be a product of chance, evolved from an unthinking, unfeeling, primordial ooze. If evolution were true, while we might be domesticated, life would only make sense being lived wild. After all, life fought to be, so we should too. To be frank, anyone who wants me to live any other way than unfettered is trying to rob me of my one, conscious life. We should be selfish, fearless, unhindered, and unrestrained. No one should stop us from living this one life that has accidentally been put before us. *What we should not be is moral. Morality only exists in a God centered paradigm.*

Those who are atheists and believe themselves to be moral are bigger fools than they think I am. I have reason to follow laws and live for others; they do not. They are literally robbing the most important and central aspect of their existence: self.

Unless, of course, there is more!

If in the end, I am wrong and the atheist is right, they would not even know it. I will die living and believing in a great hope. I will go to sleep in that rest, never knowing I was wrong. That is a wonderful way to die. The atheist however, will live a life without hope and die a life without hope. Unlike me, if they are wrong, they will know it. That is a terrible way to die.

MAGNIFICENT PURPOSE, DIVINELY CREATED

"Therefore do not seek to understand in order to believe, but believe that thou mayest understand."

- St. Augustine

Is God a great fairy tale? Ask everyone changed in the heart, healed in the spirit, and transformed in the mind by the power of the gospel. To us, we *know* something to be true. We once were lost, hurting, and broken. We were filled with sin, evil, and depravity. In a moment, after trusting by faith in Christ's sacrifice on the cross, we were different... changed...reborn. We were given new hearts and new minds and were made alive. The oldness of our ways and the deadness of our past were transformed. We were given eyes to finally see, ears to finally hear, and hearts to finally feel. Maybe that is not enough to some people, but then again, faith will always have a measure of trust within it.

We are proof though. Every one of us...every last one.

People may counter with the failings and evils of religion, because it is far easier to attack the whole and to group every religious person together. It is far easier to do this, because it is impersonal and because, in a large enough group, critics will always find enough to complain about or reject. They will always find a hypocrite to give them an excuse. It is far easier to reject religion, where unregenerate men hide, than to contend with those born of God's spirit. The evidence of the powerful and radical change in the soul of the new man is difficult to challenge. The alcoholics are made sober; the murderers made holy; the defilers made pure; the rebellious made lawful; the dishonest now with integrity; the fearful made courageous; the unfaithful now living true; the hateful now able to love; the bitter finally made free to forgive; the angry made gentle, and the wicked reborn.

It will always be easier to discredit and consequently dismiss a whole group than to deal with that friend who has suddenly become different or that coworker or employee who is not like everyone else.

I'll take the power of the gospel and its ability to change the heart of man any day. I'll take the hope in a better tomorrow and the promise of a future where this world was not for naught. I'll take the belief in a divine Creator who orders my days and guides my paths. I'll take the love of a beautiful Savior who went to the cross to save me personally, even as He saw my face in the crowd yelling, "Crucify!" I'll take the knowledge that one day all the wrong will be made right and that good will finally triumph completely and fully over evil. I'll take the belief in the God of heaven and earth who did not hold back what was most precious to Him—to redeem His enemy and the outcast—to redeem you and me.

What a powerful story it is. In this life, it births a newness of soul and, in the next, a promise fulfilled. In the end, I know that my life will be one of purpose, hope, healing, perseverance, strength, and goodness.

I will take that transforming work and all that comes with believing by faith- even the mocking, persecution, ridicule, and shaming. I will take it all- until my eyes close here and reopen there.

Until then, be blessed.

"For a day in your courts is better than a thousand elsewhere. I would rather be a doorkeeper in the house of my God than dwell in the tents of wickedness."[154]

---

154   Psalm 84:10 (ESV)

THE WRAP UP

"Or do you despise the riches of His goodness, forbearance, and longsuffering, not knowing that the goodness of God leads you to repentance?"[155]

---

[155]   Romans 2:4 (NKJV)

THE BIBLE DECLARES THAT...

Eternal life exists.

There is a judgement for everyone.

There is a personal/eternal payment for every wrong done.

Now consider that...

You are guilty.

You died tonight.

Where would you go?

THE GOSPEL

God has given man His divine law as the standard by which we can know right from wrong. The requirement of the law is perfection in thought, word and deed. So I ask you, in regards to God's law, to consider where you would be if you died tonight? Have you ever lied, even one time? Jesus said that "...all liars shall have their part in the lake which burns with fire and brimstone."[156] How about lust? Matthew 5:28 says, "But I say to you that everyone who looks at a woman with lust for her has already committed adultery with her in his heart."[157] Have you ever looked with lust? Have you ever coveted or taken God's name in vain (used God's name flippantly or with disrespect)? God said that, "the Lord will not hold him guiltless who takes his name in vain."[158] If you have broken even one of those commandments, you

---

156   Revelation 21:8 (NKJV)

157   Matthew 5:28 (NASB)

158   Exodus 20:7 (ESV)

are guilty against God's law (James 2:10). God also looks at sins of the heart like hatred (1 John 3:15), gossip (Proverbs 6:16-19), and pride (Proverbs 16:5, Mark 7:20-23). Have you ever felt or had them? James 4:17 says, "So whoever knows the right thing to do and fails to do it, for him it is sin."[159] Have you ever refused to do good when you knew it was the right thing to do?

Those are just some of the standards by which God will judge man. If You died today, knowing God's standard is perfection, and you stood before Him, would you be innocent or guilty? If you are guilty, where would you go: heaven or hell?

If you said hell, does that concern you?

If it doesn't, it should!

If it does concern you, there is hope! Two thousand years ago, God became man in the person of Jesus Christ. He lived a sinless and perfect life, fulfilling the law that we do not. He was crucified on the cross and died and then 3 days later rose again from the grave bodily, defeating death. Jesus took on Himself the punishment that we deserved. The Bible said the wrath of God fell upon Jesus to pay the price for our sins.

When Jesus rose from the dead 1) He proved that He is God and 2) He has power over death. His death satisfied the debt we owed paying in full the requirement of the Law. When we believe in Jesus Christ for salvation, all our sins are washed away—past, present, and future. Jesus takes our fine and gives us His perfect life, so when we stand before

159　James 4:17 (ESV)

God, He sees Jesus before us and we are welcomed into His presence.

If you recognize you are a sinner and realize that judgement awaits you, then turn to Christ in faith and believe the Gospel. Repent of your sins and unbelief, and put your faith and trust in Jesus Christ and Him alone for the salvation of your soul. Repentance acknowledges your guilt before God. It is a decision of the will and mind to turn away from a life of sin, rebellion, and unbelief, by the power and leading of the Holy Spirit, and turn toward Christ in faith. I also believe that repentance is an act that renounces our heritage as children of sin as we are active participants in sin by choice.

Acts 4:12 says, "And there is salvation in no one else; for there is no other name under heaven that has been given among men by which we must be saved."[160] Entrust your soul to Jesus. He alone is able to save you and free you eternally. Forgiveness is a free gift offered to everyone who turns to Christ in faith. *"For by grace you have been saved through faith; and that not of yourselves, it is the gift of God; not as a result of works, so that no one may boast."*[161] Belief in Jesus is an active choice. It is an ascent of the heart, mind, soul, and will in faith and belief in Jesus Christ, who He is, and what He did for you on the cross.

Romans 9:16 says, *"So then it is not of him who wills, nor of him who runs, but of God who shows mercy."* [162] To be certain, the Lord alone has the power to save and free man. The genuineness and truth of our faith is known to the Lord. He receives our faith, frees us from the debt we

---

160   Acts 4:12 (NASB)

161   Ephesians 2:8-9 (NASB)

162   Romans 9:16 (NKJV)

owe, and imparts His righteousness on our soul. He does it all.

In the end, it is God's goodness that heals the man of his rebellion and that man who must acknowledge that rebellion exists. When he does, God is there waiting to restore and to forgive. Those who come to understand this truth, come to a place of worship for God's mercy and forgiveness, given despite our rebellion. Worship is the expression of thankfulness and praise in the mind, the spirit, and the heart rendered to God. It is rooted in God's love for us and reflected through our worship of Him.

LOSS AND GAIN

The world, the devil, and even desire want us to feel like we lose out by turning to Christ. But what we gain is maximally greater than the brokenness we turn away from. Jackie Hill Perry said of her decision to turn to Christ from a life of sin, "*God loved me more. So much so that he wouldn't have me going about the rest of my life convinced that a creature's love was better than a King's.*"[163] Often, in God's goodness, He causes us to see that even when we fulfill our desires, we are still left feeling empty and incomplete. This is how Solomon felt:

> "*I said to myself, "Come now, I will test you with pleasure. So enjoy yourself." And behold, it too was futility. I said of laughter, "It is madness," and of pleasure, "What does it accomplish?" I explored with my mind how to stimulate my body with wine while my mind was guiding me wisely and how to take hold of folly, until I could see what*

---

163   https://www.christianitytoday.com/ct/2018/september/jackie-hill-perry-gay-girl-good-god.html Accessed November 2018

good there is for the sons of men to do under heaven the few years of their lives. I enlarged my works: I built houses for myself, I planted vineyards for myself; I made gardens and parks for myself and I planted in them all kinds of fruit trees; I made ponds of water for myself from which to irrigate a forest of growing trees. I bought male and female slaves and I had homeborn slaves. Also I possessed flocks and herds larger than all who preceded me in Jerusalem. Also, I collected for myself silver and gold and the treasure of kings and provinces. I provided for myself male and female singers and the pleasures of men—many concubines.

Then I became great and increased more than all who preceded me in Jerusalem. My wisdom also stood by me. All that my eyes desired I did not refuse them. I did not withhold my heart from any pleasure, for my heart was pleased because of all my labor and this was my reward for all my labor. Thus I considered all my activities which my hands had done and the labor which I had exerted, **and behold all was vanity and striving after wind and there was no profit under the sun.**"[164]

It is true that after salvation, we are called to pursue a holy life that is led by and obedient to Jesus—a life that is no longer led by our sinful desires. It also is true that they no longer master and control us. We are no longer held in their bondage and captive to them. We are no longer identified or defined by them. We are finally free. We also are no longer under the power and weight of sin and its punishments or our past and its guilt, shame, and regrets. In Christ, we do lose a great deal: sin, inner darkness, and spiritual death.

---

164   Ecclesiastes 2:1-11 (NASB)

What we gain in Jesus is wholeness and restoration, things that we search our entire lives to find. While this is not all we gain, they are the most powerful aspects of our new lives. Wholeness of self and, most importantly, restoration with God. From this place, everything in our life can finally heal and have purpose. Our identity then is set and no longer defined by fickle man, worldly pursuits, or our past, but instead by our Maker who knows us best and loves us most. A God who makes beauty from ashes.

When I think about the Lord, what captures and moves me the most is His beauty. I am not speaking of a physical attribute but of the nature of His person. He *is* beautiful! His ways, mind, grace, love, design, wisdom, all of it are beautiful. His heart is pure, just, and good. Despite all the ways we reject Him, He lovingly pursues us. This is what is most beautiful about salvation. Our greatest gain is Jesus!

"Come to Me, all you who labor and are heavy laden, and I will give you rest. Take My yoke upon you and learn from Me, for I am gentle and lowly in heart, and you will find rest for your souls. For My yoke is easy and My burden is light."[165]

"...it is appointed for man to die once, and after that comes judgment. so Christ, having been offered once to bear the sins of many, will appear a second time, not to deal with sin but to save those who are eagerly waiting for him."[166]

---

165 Matthew 11:28-30 (NKJV)
166 Hebrews 9:27-28 (ESV)

PART 3:

ADDITIONAL EVIDENCE

PAIN AND SUFFERING: A TESTIMONY OF GOD'S WISDOM

"Mark then, Christian, Jesus does not suffer so as to exclude your suffering. He bears a cross, not that you may escape it, but that you may endure it. Christ exempts you from sin, but not from sorrow. Remember that, and expect to suffer."[167]

"God is too good to be unkind and He is too wise to be mistaken. And when we cannot trace His hand, we must trust His heart."[168]

Charles Spurgeon

---

167   C. H. Spurgeon, Morning and Morning (New York: Sheldon and Company, 1865), April 5, p. 96

168   https://www.google.com/amp/s/www.crosswalk.com/faith/spiritual-life/inspiring-quotes/20-powerful-quotes-from-charles-spurgeon.html%3famp=1 Accessed October 2018

People often ask why God allows pain and suffering. One thing I realized early in my life was that there is a redemptive purpose in both of them. I am not trying to diminish the reality of the sadness and brokenness that accompanies life's trials, but they are not without divine purpose. No one ever likes to enter a season of pain, but everyone is changed as a result of the experience.

LIBERATOR

Our minds naturally get clouded by everything that surrounds us. Materialism often is what we chase and use to identify worth in others and ourselves. The idea that possession equals value is reinforced everywhere we look and binds us to the realm of the superficial.

The desires of the world are only magnified with the addition of the digital age. There is constant pressure to fit in and amass "likes" and views. Social media has led to increased want, vanity, pride, and frivolous pursuits. Additionally, we get lost for hours in a world of internet illusions, at times forgetting those most important to us.

When pain and suffering enter, everything changes. Pain is a great liberator. It has the ability to remove us from the veil of materialism that shadows this world and that often enslaves us as people. When we are going through a difficulty, it allows us to distinguish what is truly important from what is trivial. Most importantly, in our culture of worldliness and excess, pain awakens us and causes us to look up and consider God.

Often when pain enters, we realize that everything we thought really mattered is actually insignificant. We stop worrying about keeping in step with cultural norms and expectations, and we begin to focus on the most precious things.

When Instagram blogger Kyrzayda Rodriguez died, her last post before her death went viral. It highlighted that toward the end, her possessions were unimportant. The knowledge of her impending death allowed her to recognize what was most precious to her:

"I have a brand new car parked outside that can't do anything for me, I have all kinds of designers clothes, shoes, and bags that can't do anything for me, I have money in my account that can't do anything for me, I have a big well-furnished house that can't do anything for me.

Look, I'm lying here in a twin size hospital bed; I can take a plane any day of the week if I like but that can't do anything for me.... So do not let anyone make u feel bad for the things you don't have—but the things u have, be happy with those; if you have a roof over your head who cares what kind of furniture is in it....the most important thing in life is LOVE.[169]

When we are facing death, suffering, or going through a painful experience, life is more real, and our true purpose is less clouded. We no longer run after the wrong pursuits. It also helps us to seek out healing in our broken relationships, sometimes after years of estrangement from our loved ones.

Pain and suffering also bring clarity to who God is and why we are here. Often it allows us to pray genuinely to God and to seek Him out

---

169   https://www.standardmedia.co.ke/evewoman/article/2001296407/the-last-words-of-kyrzayda-rodriguez-famous-fashion-blogger-who-succumbed-to-cancer Accessed October 2018

beyond our imaginations of Him. It severs the loosely defined image that we have and calls us to question who He really is. It is often pain and suffering that bring someone in rebellion to a place of surrender, leading them to saving faith in Jesus Christ. His goodness meets us even when we are furthest from Him and most in need of Him. This is God's wisdom.

REFINER

While uncomfortable, pain has a great purpose. It illuminates our sin, exposes our weaknesses, and points us towards God. The Lord frequently uses pain and difficulty to remove what is wrong within us and to create in us what we are lacking. This is the refining of our soul. We are told in Scripture of the refiner's fire that purges away sin and leaves beauty in its place. I imagine that our sins and bondages are so entwined within us, that only fire has the ability to remove them. I know my love for sin has often only been removed because of God's heavy hand on my soul. On the other side of the refiner's fire is strength of faith and character that is stronger than the love for the sin and bondage that once held me captive.

In 2 Corinthians 12:7-10, Paul's experience of suffering was used by God to keep him from exalting himself and to realize God's power in his weakness. Despite Paul's asking God three times to remove his thorn in the flesh, the Lord instead caused Paul to see His faithfulness throughout his trial. Paul learned greater faith through every pain and suffering that the Lord brought his way.

This is the case for countless followers of Jesus. We may face a multitude of difficulties in our life, and in every circumstance we learn how real the Lord is and how precious are His promises. Whether we recognize God's hand in the trial or see His hand afterwards, we know that we only made it through because God was faithful to us.

Lastly, pain and suffering define us as people. There are countless individuals who truly began to live as a result of the very pain and suffering that they faced. They are people who refused to allow the trials to shake them. Often, courage is magnified through endurance and resilience. Strength of spirit glorifies God as we see the determination of the human spirit that He created. It is a testimony of God's created design.

RENOUNCING EASE

We desire ease and a life without any difficulty. But great faith and strong character are never built on the back of comfort. This also is God's wisdom. In the Bible, we see periods of persecution (Paul), illness (Job), wilderness (Moses), separation (John the Baptist), threats of death (Elijah), and fleeing from oppressors (David) from God's mightiest warriors. Out of pain and suffering came a definite fortitude.

Going through pain and suffering removes the deadly sins of pride and self-righteousness from our spirit, allowing us to learn compassion and humility. At the same time, the trials we go through help us to come alongside others when they are in pain. They help mold our humanity into one of gentleness and sympathy. We see this truth in 2 Corinthians 1:3-4, "*Blessed be the God and Father of our Lord Jesus*

Christ, the Father of mercies and God of all comfort, who comforts us in all our affliction, so that we may be able to comfort those who are in any affliction, with the comfort with which we ourselves are comforted by God.[170] We are given the gift of sympathy and empathy that allows us to consider another person's pain. But how could we appropriately join another's pain without understanding our own through personal experience? God has designed us as social creatures with the purpose of community. Entering into the pain and suffering of another is one of the greatest characteristics that defines our humanity. It also is one of the most beautiful and valiant components of our life on this earth. The intimacy that is brought from tragedy is birthed from pain and suffering. It has the ability to break through boundaries of religion, gender, sex, culture, and generation. It calls us toward the need of another. This is the wisdom of God.

We should not run from pain and suffering. We should not see it as a mistake of God but rather what it was designed to be—a tool to draw one soul to another. In this aspect, it is perfect and effective.

As a believer, pain and suffering also has taught me about the enemies of fear, worry, doubt, unbelief, and impatience. Through moments of utter brokenness, I have seen God the clearest and have seen every way that my life has needed His entrance. My pain has been a mirror to my soul and my need like no other tool outside of repentance.

Pain and suffering may not be enjoyable, but it is one of the most human aspects of this existence. There is no greater tool other than

170   2 Cor 1:3-4 (ESV)

love, which has the power to unite a soul to another and to heal what has been broken by sin. This too is the wisdom of God.

"O dear friend, when thy grief presses thee to the very dust, worship there!"

Charles Spurgeon

THE GOD WE ARE NOT

ARGUMENT FROM DESIGN

"I am God, and there is no other; I am God, and there is none like me."[171]

SOPHIA, MAN'S ADAM

Sophia, the artificial intelligence (AI) designed by Hanson Robotics, was granted citizenship to Saudi Arabia in 2017. She is the first robot ever to have a nationality. She is an intricately and beautifully designed "social humanoid," developed by a team of brilliant men and women who worked on "her" for the past 12+ years.

Hanson's chief scientist, Ben Goertzel, has spoken in detail about Sophia's technology. She consists of "face tracking, emotion recognition, and robotic movements generated by deep neural networks. Although most of Sophia's dialogue comes from a simple decision tree (the same tech used by chatbots; when you say X, it replies Y), what it says is integrated with these other inputs in a unique fashion."[172] "She is able to simulate more than 60 different facial expressions, track and recognise faces, look people in the eye, and hold natural conversations. And she appears even more human-like thanks to a material that mimics real human musculature and skin that allows her to seem more expressive."[173] To operate Sophia, the designers use three different systems of control: "1) a purely script-based "timeline editor," which is used for preprogrammed speeches, and occasionally for media interactions that come with prespecified questions; 2) a 'sophisticated chat-bot'—that chooses from a large palette of templatized responses based on context and a limited level of understanding (and that also sometimes gives a response grabbed from an online resource, or generated stochastically).

---

172 https://www.theverge.com/2017/11/10/16617092/sophia-the-robot-citizen-ai-han-son-robotics-ben-goertzel Accessed 14 October 2018

173 https://www.dailymail.co.uk/sciencetech/article-5251185/Worlds-robot-citizen-Sophia-gets-legs.html Accessed 14 October 2018

3) OpenCog, a sophisticated cognitive architecture created with AGI in mind. It is still in R&D, but it is already being used for practical value in some domains, such as biomedical informatics, see *Mozi Health* and a bunch of SingularityNET applications to be rolled out this fall."[174]

The intelligence behind the development of Sophia is so sophisticated that their designer comments that when discussing it, people do not have an idea what he is talking about. "If I tell people I'm using probabilistic logic to do reasoning on how best to prune the backward chaining inference trees that arise in our logic engine, they have no idea what I'm talking about. But if I show them a beautiful smiling robot face, then they get the feeling that AGI may indeed be nearby and viable."[175]

Despite the brilliance behind her development, her designers are clear that she is not "alive." "Digital and robotic entities are not the same as biological entities, so applying words like 'alive' to them often is going to be more misleading than informative....Currently, the Sophia robot—and all other existing robots—lack the kinds of independence and autonomy that are characteristic of biological lifeforms."[176] While her designers believe that they can develop her to a place where she is more of an independent system, they acknowledge that biological life is not a possibility. "Of course even if we get a robot like this to truly

---

174   http://hplusmagazine.com/2017/11/05/sophia-singularitynet-qa/ Accessed 14 October 2018

175   https://www.theverge.com/2017/11/10/16617092/sophia-the-robot-citizen-ai-hanson-robotics-ben-goertzel Accessed 14 October 2018

176   http://hplusmagazine.com/2017/11/05/sophia-singularitynet-qa/ Accessed 14 October 2018

merit citizenship in a Western-style democracy, and win 100 Nobel Prizes, that still won't make it "alive" in the exact sense that a biological system is. Its internal physical mechanisms won't have the adaptive and self-organizing nature of human cells."[177]

As for her future development, Goertzel said, "During the next year we will be progressively incorporating more and more of OpenCog's learning and reasoning algorithms into this 'Hanson AI' framework, along with various AI agents running on the SingularityNET decentralized AI-meets-blockchain framework. Along with more sophisticated use of PLN, and better modeling of human-like emotional dynamics and their impact on cognition, we will also be incorporating cognition-driven stochastic language generation, using language models inferred by our novel *unsupervised grammar induction algorithms*. And so much more."[178]

UNLIKE ADAM

Due to evolution's divorce of the belief in God and the existence of the soul, we have diminished the complexity of humanness and the uniqueness of life. If we merely evolved by chance and randomness, then we would be easily reproducible. Afterall if chance can bring about life from nonlife, then complex creatures, such as modern man, surely can do the same. Randomness and chance is not thinking or

---

177   http://hplusmagazine.com/2017/11/05/sophia-singularitynet-qa/ Accessed 14 October 2018

178   http://www.hansonrobotics.com/how-sophia-the-robot-works-goertzel/ Accessed 14 October 2018

purposeful, and yet here we are. Clearly, we are better than randomness and chance.

Creationist Phil Snider noted that, *"One of the problems with Darwinian evolution is that it requires there to have been multiplied millions of upward increases in life complexity; however, this has never been demonstrated or even observed."* He further noted that *"human effort is dozens or even hundreds of orders of magnitude more efficient than chance"* and yet despite all our advancements, we are incapable of creating biological life from nothing. We are incapable of doing what chance has done despite being maximally more efficient than chance.

We are at a place in history where our knowledge is allowing us to study the universe and its beginnings. We have inventions that allow us to communicate real time in a different language and self-driving electric cars. We have 3-D printing, virtual worlds, the ability to clone, robotic eyes, and we can even do full-face transplants. We are clearly intelligent people.

We have the knowledge to build a human-looking robot and the intelligence to trigger the uncanny valley response, yet we do not have the judgement to connect the obvious dots. *This is the difference between knowledge and wisdom.*

How is it possible to have robots, who by necessity, were created by brilliant people with the thinking, reasoning, awareness, and capability to design, program, and correct their development, yet assume we are here accidentally through chance and randomness? With the ingenuity and thought behind a robot like Sophia, there exists people who have worked countless years on her development and are still researching ways to make her more "alive." As it stands now, she is arguably the most impressive of the AI robots, yet is no more than a glorified chatbot with special features.

Yet unlike Sophia, man is so much more than mimicry, programming, and time. We are by creation, greater, deeper, and more than mere movement and mechanics. While impressive, Sophia will never be what mankind is. This is the foolishness of a world without a belief in God. We have rejected that man is far beyond the brain, chemical processes, and makeup of our DNA. Those are indeed the mechanics of our body, but beyond that we have the actuality of a soul. We have the existence of a unique quality to life that is not programmed, it is. We do not just learn morality, we *are* moral. We are not just programmed to exist, we *are* alive. Our soul is the depth that causes us to reason and love, to ponder and sacrifice, and to question and imagine. Our soul is so beyond explanation that we can barely qualify it. Every statement we give of it falls wildly short of what it is. This is why we could never create one; we can hardly describe it to do so. All we know is that it is. No matter how well you design a robot, you can never bring forth a soul. Aristotle wrote that *"the knowledge of the soul admittedly contributes greatly to the advance of truth in general, and, above all, to our understanding of nature."*[179] How right he was. Modern man is incredibly intelligent, yet shockingly ignorant.

---

179 Adler, Mortimer. The Great ideas, A Syntopicon 2, Man to World. William Benton, 1952

COPYCATS

This is the argument from design. It is a powerful argument that recognizes that what we create requires a creator. Its logic is so simple that to argue it is intellectual dishonesty. If purposeful, intelligent thought and design goes into the development of a car, a plane, or even a toaster. Why would we believe that this universe and all it contains is any different? Are we really less complex than a toaster?

The design of Sophia is born from the tools already present and known. We took God's design and His handiwork and are trying to write our name on it like it is ours. It is akin to someone taking a masterpiece like the Mona Lisa and signing their own name on the reproduction. I can call it whatever I want but we all know who the real artist is.

In all our advancements the creation of biological life from sheer nothingness will always be an impossibility, no matter how much time is allowed to pass. The foolishness of this thought is witnessed in Sophia. She is evidence that God exists. A God of thought, beauty, design, purpose, intelligence with personhood, and desire for communication with His creation. As all those things were necessary to bring her about and were purposed in her development, is the same necessity for our own. She is evolutionists' greatest problem, and yet she is maximally less complex than biological life. While we have learned so much about this creation, we have not even touched the surface of the mind and intelligence of God.

As long as we continue to reject God, our culture will never be greater than a one-dimensional life and surface-level existence. Everything from morality, purpose, and man's definite intrinsic value is defined and established by God. To be anti-God is to attack the realm of the soul and the substance of man. It is time that we as a people recognize that atheism is no more than a religion of rejection whose God is science and savior is man. Their claims of the origins of life are protected by prophets who refuse to acknowledge the evidence of God. Their ardent partiality calls to question their sagacity. As evolutionary biologist Richard Lewontin stated, *"Materialism is absolute, for we cannot allow a Divine foot in the door."*[180]

"I am an atheist. My attitude is not based on science, but rather on faith.... The absence of a Creator, the nonexistence of God is my childhood faith, my adult belief, unshakable and holy."[181]

George Klein

---

180   Lewontin, R. 1997. Billions and Billions of Demons.

181   Klein, G. 1990. *The Atheist in the Holy City.*

EVIDENCE OF ARTISTRY AND CRAFTSMANSHIP

MORE ARGUMENTS FROM DESIGN

"Beauty is what makes God, God. God is God, and distinguished from all other beings, and exalted above them, chiefly by his divine beauty. Not sovereignty, not wrath, not grace, not omniscience, not eternity, but beauty is what more than anything else defines God's very divinity."

Jonathan Edwards

ARTISTRY

"Always personal, always original, interpretation is the art of transforming an idea into matter. In the process, the one who interprets is much like a translator, a negotiator or a mediator, drawing on an extensive base of knowledge, sensitivity and understanding to shape one reality into another. As interpreter, the master artisan harvests and makes sense of things to allow the beautiful, the original, the personal and the useful to emerge harmoniously."[182]

The Michelangelo Foundation for Creativity and Craftsmanship seeks to "celebrate and preserve master craftsmanship and strengthen its connection to the world of design."[183] The nonprofit foundation believes that "creating a shared definition of excellence allows us to recognise and honour mastery and set a standard to which artisans of every age, specialty and country can aspire." They use an 11-point criteria to designate a master craftsman: Authenticity, Competence, Craftsmanship, Creativity, Innovation, Interpretation, Originality, Talent, Territory, Tradition, Training.

One of the clearest evidence of God that is present and observable all around us is the existence of artistry and craftsmanship throughout creation. Every point of criteria that designates a master craftsman is witnessed or birthed in the creation of our world, showing that a reasoning mind is behind its existence. There is not a place on this globe where creation has not been touched by these disciplines. The

---

182   https://www.michelangelofoundation.org/criteria-for-excellence/interpretation/   Accessed November 2018

183   https://www.michelangelofoundation.org/the-foundation/ Accessed November 2018

quality of craftsmanship and artistry are beyond simple and ordinary; they are the attribution of a master artist.

There is no singleness or plainness to God's design. Wherever God's hands have been, we witness an explosion of artistry displayed in mixed textures, patterns, and layers, the use of different mediums, careful placements, and measurements throughout, the existence of symmetry, the presence of different sizes and shapes, the appeal and existence of all senses, the presence of function and purpose, the use of bold and varying colors, the presence of mimicry, style, beauty, and harmony, the existence of different creatures and elements, varying modes of reproduction, excellence in form, and quality and complexity. Intelligence and uniqueness is observed throughout the universe. God's mastery of art is witnessed everywhere.

God is both the designer and man's artistic interpreter. He has brought to life the thoughts of His mind and allows man the ability to see a visible representation of His glory. Creation is breathtaking indeed. God is an architect of excellence. Difference is His signature.

No evolutionary necessity exists for variety, especially of such magnitude. A standard and simple system is all that is necessary for biological evolution and the only reasonable structure that would be produced from randomness, chance, and a purely unthinking process. Biological evolution just needs time, function, and capability, but the presence of complexity, depth, and artistic purpose is the handiwork of thought.

We are not talking about single variances either but differences in multiplatforms. Many of these design components exist at the same time, in the same created element and in layers within itself, like a designer putting together a room. This feature exists throughout the total of creation.

MASTER ARTIST

When you go to a museum you can feel the artists' emotion in their painting. This is especially true of a great artist. Their painting literally speaks to your heart and soul. You can sense the raw emotion behind their art. Artist Stephan Baumann wrote about his connection with his work: "*When I paint a painting, I am in tune with my feelings about the subject.... I look at my subject as if I was young child, seeing the subject for the first time. If you do this, you might see the world with awe and wonder, and feel the connection you have with everything around you. Feelings come from seeing what is in front of you, not just looking. Witness the texture, see the color, look for the light and shadow; enjoy these simple pleasures of sight that are often forgotten and ignored nowadays. Look at your subject with wonder, see the curves, notice the light; is it warm or cool? Feel the subject. Close your eyes, interpret it in your mind, enhance it, turn up the volume to increase the brightness, soften the edges, and add atmosphere. See it with your soul, then paint exactly what you see and feel.*"[184]

God, the master artisan, is excellent in His creation of territory—a term meaning to encompass "*a rich mixture of ideas linking an object to*

---

184   http://www.stefanbaumann.com/expressing-feeling-in-your-paintings/ Accessed November 2018

its maker and to the geophysical and social environment that shapes them both." To me, this is the distinguishing beauty that is behind God's creation of culture. Each area and people group is created to glorify God uniquely and to have their own traditions, histories, and beauty. The richness and variety of music, food, language, dance, location, and people, all hold a personal qualifying artistry.

God's creation drives men to capture the magnificence, beauty, and intensity of the known world in a medium. Art then becomes a moment of transference from the object, to you, through the artist's eyes. In the same way, we have this experience looking at a beautiful sunset, sitting at the beach watching the ocean or standing on the top of a mountain. We are moved in our spirit by what we are experiencing. We have a sense that its beauty is intentional, as if God is speaking to us through it, which He is.

Like a great painting, creation can evoke a variety of emotions, often proportionate to the mastery of work and richness behind what is being observed. It can quiet us, slow us down, or inspire us to pursue every dream. Psychiatrist Mark Goulston wrote about his first experience at the Grand Canyon: "*I can still remember my first experience of standing at the edge of the Grand Canyon and looking into it. It was so awesome; it took a fair amount of restraint to prevent me from jumping into it, because I was certain I could fly.*" This is the power of the artistry behind the Lord's created hand. It is meant to move and quiet our soul, to glorify God, and to move our mind to consider His existence.

Creation is designed to be beautiful, purposeful, and functional.

Frederick Law Olmsted, the great landscape architect wrote, *"It is a scientific fact, that the occasional contemplation of natural scenes of an impressive character—is favorable to the health and vigor of men and especially to the health and vigor of their intellect."*[185] This also is the calling of a great artist. Man is drawn to the artistry in the great landscapes as we become visitors to God's open museum. Our universe has a beauty so compelling and demonstrates an intelligence so profound that we live our whole lives being moved by its greatness. We argue about its purpose and are silenced by its magnificence. Everyone from the atheist to the Christian is in awe of it.

Like any great artist, you can feel God's emotion in His creation. As mighty as His power is, that is how beautiful His heart is. God is truly breathtaking. It causes us to ponder like the Psalmist why a God so great would ever create and care for us. *"When I look at your heavens, the work of your fingers, the moon and the stars, which you have set in place, what is man that you are mindful of him, and the son of man that you care for him?"*[186] Yet He does. This is the wisdom and beauty of God.

CRAFTSMANSHIP

"Creativity, the capacity to invent new ideas or objects, is what distinguishes an artisan from a master artisan, an object from a masterpiece, a simple task or job from embodied know-how. In fine craftsmanship, it is a dynamic force, a blend of personal vision, passion and perfect skill, able

---

185   https://www.nationalgeographic.com/magazine/2016/01/call-to-wild/ Accessed November 2018

186   Psalm 8:3-4 (ESV)

to balance functional and material limitations with invention, stretching the rules of the art to meet the imagination and respond to contemporary needs and tastes."[187]

The creativity, care, and contemplation behind creation and the particular consideration given for mankind are works of craftsmanship. There is no mark of guessing, chance, indifference, or failure in our universe. We see the handiwork of brilliance combined with the wisdom, intelligence, knowledge, artistry, and craftsmanship behind it.

The world we live in is excellent in its design. While it is fallen, it is perfectly complete and thought through. Even what is wrong within our world, due to the fall, is accounted for in the existence of its opposite. There is nothing left without thought. We have medicine derived from plants to balance illness, we have justice and law to balance sin, and we are given relationships and community to balance suffering and loneliness. Everything exists in this universe as essential components for each other, pointing to God's forethought in creation. The universe shows the mark of competence, both in the quality of its design, the successful implementation of various materials and techniques, and the conscious application of purpose.

Take nature for example. There are creatures that guarantee another's survival, such as alligators and nesting birds, creatures that have symbiotic relationships, such as crabs and venomous sea urchins and creatures that are top predators ensuring balance and order by preventing specific species from growing too large. What should be

---

187   https://www.michelangelofoundation.org/criteria-for-excellence/creativity/
Accessed November 2018

examples of chaos and failure are instead a demonstration of a mind that is both creative and original.

God likewise shows His innovation all throughout our planet. Consider flowers, such as orchids that use mimicry, trickery, and deceit to fool its pollinator. Darwin was captivated by Orchids, noting that the "inexhaustible number of contrivances by which orchids ensure their pollination, pointing out that these would have entailed changes in every part of the flower."[188] Darwin recognized the exceptional nature of the orchid, but sadly failed to see the designer behind it. Like him, evolutionists claim that the "flowers and insects have evolved simultaneously to be complementary to each other."[189] They understand principally that the flower needs the insect for its survival and recognize that each unique design requires an equally unique pollinator. However, they fail to see that the changes, adjustments, and corrections ensuring the orchids survival would require a reasoning mind. They also fail to see that the requirements of change, adjustment, and correction necessary for survival would be essential for every biological creature, requiring an impossible amount of successful, completed randoms.

Geoff Chapman wrote in his article "Orchids...A Witness to the Creator": "The intricate design of many orchids belies the idea that they slowly evolved. Since the whole purpose of their sophisticated machinery is to ensure the continuation of the species through pollination, and since without pollination the species would become

---

188   Charles Darwin, *The Origin of Species*, Mentor, New York (NY), 1958, p. 179

189   https://answersingenesis.org/biology/plants/orchids-a-witness-to-the-creator/ Accessed November 2018

extinct, it follows that every part of this apparatus needed to be in place and working right from the start. If an orchid needed to look like a bee or other insect in order to attract a pollinator, then until it bore a significant resemblance the insect would not be interested."[190] In essence, it could not survive if it was not perfectly complete. It is literally impossible.

Let me put it to you another way. Say that we were on an island where a volcano was presently going to erupt, and our life and survival depended on a helicopter flying us away to safety. If we had to wait an expanse of time for the helicopter to be created, we would die. If we had to create the helicopter while the volcano was erupting, we would die. The helicopter would have to already have been created to ensure our survival; however, in evolution, no thinking, rational creature would recognize the need to build one or have the knowledge to complete it. If by chance and randomness, the elements necessary to create a helicopter were present, what would the likelihood be of creating one, successfully, on time, without reason and thought? If all the pieces were present, but without thought and reason behind them, wouldn't it be just as likely to create a flashlight or nothing at all?

INTELLIGENT DESIGN

Intelligent design advocate William Dembski noted three necessary elements required to claim design: "*Whenever we infer design, we must establish three things: contingency, complexity, and specification.*

---

190   https://answersingenesis.org/biology/plants/orchids-a-witness-to-the-creator/ Accessed November 2018

Contingency ensures that the object in question is not the result of an automatic and therefore unintelligent process that had no choice in its production. Complexity ensures that the object is not so simple that it can readily be explained by chance. Finally specification ensures the object exhibits the type of pattern characteristic of intelligence."[191]

When you look at the orchid *coupled with* their unique pollinators, they clearly show evidence of intelligent design. Orchids are only one example. Our world is full of similar examples that fit Dembski's criteria above. Consider that machinery exists in microscopic living cells. Jonathan Sarfati of creation.com highlights this unique design in his article on germs "Germ with seven motors in one!" noting *"Over the last two decades, scientists have uncovered some of the amazing machinery in microscopic living cells. These include germs with a miniature motor that—the bacterial flagellum. This even turns out to have a clutch to disconnect the motor from the tail. Even more miniaturized is the tiniest motor in the universe, ATP synthase, which makes the vital energy molecule ATP (adenosine triphosphate). Remarkably, a virus has a tiny motor used to wind up DNA into tight packages.... Some germs have more than one flagellum. Sometimes they work individually but still the germ manages to coordinate the motors."*[192]

What's unique about these microscopic systems is the clear presence of machinery. Both complex (motors) and simple (wheels) machinery are seen in their design. The wheel, for example, "cited as the hallmark

---

191   William A. Dembski, *Intelligent Design – The Bridge Between Science & Theology* Downers Grove, IL: IVP Academic, 1999, p. 128

192   https://creation.com/germ-7-motors-in-1 Accessed December 2018

of man's innovation,"[193] traces its origins back to the bronze age. By this time in history, man was already working with metals, designing complex musical instruments, herding domesticated animals, planting crops, etc. The wheel, considered a "one hundred percent *homo sapien* innovation,"[194] was clearly created by an intelligent creature. When discussing the invention of the wheel, David Anthony, a professor of anthropology at Hartwick College, stated that "*The stroke of brilliance was the wheel-and-axle concept.... But then making it was also difficult.*" Noting further "*The sensitivity of the wheel-and-axle system to all these factors meant that it could not have been developed in phases.... It was an all-or-nothing structure.*"[195] Yet we see the existence of microscopic systems with analogous designs, raising the question of their own intelligent Creator.

Jonathan Sarfati highlights an example of this intelligent design in the fast-swimming magnetism sensing bacterium MO-1. "*The bacterial flagellum is a motility organelle that **consists of a rotary motor and a helical propeller**. The flagella usually work individually or by forming a loose bundle to produce thrust. However, the flagellar apparatus of marine bacterium MO-1 is a tight bundle of seven flagellar filaments enveloped in a sheath.... The seven filaments are enveloped with 24 fibrils in the sheath, and their basal bodies are arranged in an intertwined hexagonal array similar to the thick and thin filaments of vertebrate skeletal muscles.*

---

193   https://www.smithsonianmag.com/science-nature/a-salute-to-the-wheel-31805121/#xxrfpMkB w0I4ogff.99 Accessed December 2018

194   https://www.smithsonianmag.com/science-nature/a-salute-to-the-wheel-31805121/ Accessed December 2018

195   https://www.livescience.com/18808-invention-wheel.html Accessed December 2018

*This **complex and exquisite architecture** strongly suggests that the fibrils counter-rotate between flagella in direct contact to minimize the friction of high-speed rotation of individual flagella in the tight bundle within the sheath to enable MO-1 cells to swim at about 300 μm/s."*[196]

The research team studying the MO-1 noted, *"Although there is no direct evidence that the fibrils can rotate freely in the opposite direction as the flagellar filaments with which they are in direct contact, we think this is the simplest interpretation to explain the **superior function** afforded by the **complex architecture** of the MO-1 flagellar apparatus. Considering the very tight packing of the 7 flagella and 24 fibrils that are in direct physical contact within the sheath, there appears to be no other way for the flagella to rotate at high speed without the counter rotation of the intervening fibrils."*[197] The MO-1 bacterium clearly fits Dembski's criteria for intelligent design, demonstrating contingency, complexity, and specification in its structure.

THE CRAFTSMAN

noun, plural crafts·men.

1. a person who practices or is highly skilled in a craft; artisan.

2. an artist.[198]

My Uncle Curtis is a master carpenter. His work is always beautiful and never without great attention and purpose. There is a marked difference in the work he produces and the work a "do it yourselfer"

---

196   http://www.pnas.org/content/109/50/20643 Accessed December 2018

197   http://www.pnas.org/content/109/50/20643 Accessed December 2018

198   https://www.dictionary.com/browse/craftsman Accessed November 2018

puts out. There is a level of skill and a quality that comes from his 30+ years in the business. Whether he is working on a contract or doing something in his home, he will not settle for mediocracy. He strives for perfection and considers the needs and desires of the person for whom he is designing. He will not present a product to someone unless it is complete and excellent. My uncle is a true craftsman.

In the same manner, Walt Harrington, in his book: "Acts of Creation: America's Finest Hand Craftsmen at Work" profiled other great American craftsman and found that they "strive to approach perfection, envisioning it, aiming for it, and then mastering the possibilities and limits of tools and materials...."[199] The craftsmen are the artists of their trade. Their work is recognized by the quality, detail, and thought behind their medium. One thing is true of all: perfection is their goal.

There is something definable about the work of a great artist or craftsman. It is hard to put in words other than to say that you will know their work when you see it. If you are in a room full of average or mass produced craft, the exceptional will always stop you in your tracks. Oftentimes, it will take your breath away.

Ludovic Avenel, craftsman cabinetmaker, said, "*When we make something with our hands, we can tweak it until we achieve the result we are looking for.... And when we do it with passion and pleasure, we*

---

199   https://www.craftsmanshipmuseum.com/HarringtonCraftsmanship.htm
     Accessed November 2018

transfer a part of ourselves into this object."[200] I believe this is why we stop and recognize the exceptional, something about it speaks that it was made with more than cursory thought and average skill. The mastery is evident.

This is analogous to the craftsmanship and emotion behind man's particular design. We uniquely bear God's image and are the purposeful work of His hands. The greatest care and beauty went into the genesis of man. We demonstrate the mark of God's excellence and are the proof of a master craftsman. "*For you formed my inward parts; you knitted me together in my mother's womb. I praise you, for I am fearfully and wonderfully made. Wonderful are your works; my soul knows it very well. My frame was not hidden from you, when I was being made in secret, intricately woven in the depths of the earth. Your eyes saw my unformed substance; in your book were written, every one of them, the days that were formed for me, when as yet there was none of them.*"[201]

Beyond man lies an incalculable amount of created things that also bear the mark of brilliance. God is indeed glorified in all His work.

We read in Isaiah 64:8 "*But now, O LORD, you are our Father; we are the clay, and you are our potter; we are all the work of your hand.*"[202]Colossians 1:15-17 says, Jesus "*is the image of the invisible God, the firstborn over all creation. For by Him all things were created that are in heaven and that are on earth, visible and invisible, whether thrones or*

---

200   https://www.michelangelofoundation.org/criteria-for-excellence/craftsmanship/   Accessed November 2018

201   Psalm 139:13-16 (ESV)

202   Isaiah 64:8 (ESV)

dominions or principalities or powers. All things were created through Him *and for Him. And He is before all things, and in Him all things consist.*" Lastly, in Job 33:4, we read of the Holy Spirit: "*The Spirit of God has* *made me, And the breath of the Almighty gives me life.*"

All three persons of the trinity are responsible for the creation of the universe and the excellence we see demonstrated throughout. Our universe establishes the fact of an unparalleled genius behind its origin as what is present in creation could not come without thought, precision, wisdom, and a powerful, intelligent cause. Additionally, the presence of artistry and craftsmanship is a testament that the intelligent cause is a personal One that has emotion, life, and passion.

Ray Comfort put it so well when he said, "*Atheists who keep asking* *for evidence of God's existence are like a fish in the ocean wanting evidence* *of water.*" How true this is, the evidence for God is truly everywhere!

"*But now ask the beasts, and let them teach you; and the birds of the* *heavens, and let them tell you. Or speak to the earth, and let it teach you;* *and let the fish of the sea declare to you. Who among all these does not know* *that the hand of the Lord has done this; In whose hand is the life of every* *living thing, and the breath of all mankind?*"[203]

---

203 Job 12:7-10 (NASB)

SOMETHING FROM
SOMEONE

"The safest truth is the simplest"[204]

C. H. Spurgeon

---

204   https://www.girdedwithtruth.org/spurgeon-quotes-on-truth-1/ Accessed October 2018

When we look at our world, we recognize that things exist that are beyond the possibility of evolutionary origin. The existence of these "things" are unique and often found within humankind alone. For example, we observe that personhood, wisdom, spoken language, morality, truth, logic, and self-consciousness exist. These qualities are complex and are the byproducts of thought and intelligence. Additionally, for the most part, they are unnecessary from the standpoint of evolution. For instance, biological evolution and the necessity of survival can exist without transcendent logic and personhood. Yet, we see that these things exist. Their reality requires a cause sufficient for their existence. In addition to a sufficient cause, they require a capability for their existence and an awareness of their necessity.

Unlike the argument from biological evolution that claims complexity through time, the nature of these "things" merit a cause beyond mere evolution and time. These are qualities that are endowed, not evolved. For example, wisdom is required for wisdom, morality for morality, etc. Some may argue that these are observable truths but that would require the intelligence to recognize their significance, the knowledge to apply them, and the wisdom to establish them. Most importantly, it would require one to observe to consider their need and a prior observable "thing." Clearly, one cannot observe morality without a moral object to observe. The flowchart below further illustrates my point. I recognize these are "things" grammatically, under the position of nouns.

SOMETHING FROM SOMEONE

- Nothing cannot bring forth something.

- From nothing, comes nothing.

- Some things exist.

- Therefore, something came from something.

- That something must contain or have knowledge of what it brings forth.

- As something cannot bring forth what it lacks in knowledge, awareness, or possession.

- Therefore, that something must contain authority, personhood, life, emotion, knowledge, intelligence, spoken language, awareness, wisdom, goodness, justice, truth, morality, logic, and beauty.

- Because those things exist.

- Therefore, they came from something.

- That something by necessity must be someone.

- As what it contains defines a One not a thing.

- By necessity, someone is greater in being and knowledge than what He brings forth and possesses.

- Therefore, that someone is a maximally great someone as He brought forth maximally great things.

- A maximally great someone by necessity must be God.

- As only God is a maximally great someone.

- Therefore, because these things exist, by necessity God exists.

DIVINE ORIGINS

Many of the origins of the qualities above have been argued since early man walked the earth. However, without God as the beginner, there can never be an explanation for their existence. The existence of these "things" require their possibility, their possibility requires capability, their capability requires awareness, awareness requires knowledge, knowledge requires wisdom, and wisdom requires One who is wise as wisdom is thinking. Evolution alone can never account for them.

When considering the existence of the qualities above coupled with a universe with apparent excellence for survival, universally completed applications of life and the obvious presence of design, artistry, and craftsmanship, a God-created universe is the only reasonable explanation. Furthermore, when you recognize that organic survival through the process of biological evolution would by necessity, require an extraordinary amount of upward perfections, and completion occurrences through an unintelligent, random chance process, it is clearly impossible.

To be more specific, it is not just biological evolution of man alone that we are considering but the evolution of every living creature, every non-sentient organic being, and every biological existence would have had to come to perfect completion immediately for its survival. This would be every inorganic material contained in this universe; every perfected element within our universe (i.e., gravity, rotation, and placement of the earth and planets); every transcendent existence of law and logic; every aspect of humanity and the listed "things" above; every characteristic of soul, such as reasoning and self-awareness— everything evolved randomly from chance, absent of any thought, correction, knowledge, or intelligence. If anything stands without evidence, it is that worldview.

God has given us a brain, and He calls us to use it. While the understanding of His existence is challenging and requires faith, it is maximally more probable than chance. Especially when you take into account that the protectors of the atheistic worldview have clearly shown an obvious disdain to a God they supposedly do not believe in, many admitting that they refuse to even "allow a divine foot in the door." What we are looking at is people with an obvious bias and an absolute refusal to examine evidence that is contrary to their unbelief. That is something that should be considered when we are questioning our existence and the validity of their claims.

"Man fallaciously says, 'I think, therefore, I am'; but God says, 'I AM, therefore, you think."

Jason Lisle

Therefore Pilate said to Him, "So You are a king?" Jesus answered, "You say correctly that I am a king. For this I have been born, and for this I have come into the world, to testify to the truth. Everyone who is of the truth hears My voice. Pilate said to Him,

WHAT IS TRUTH?[205]

"He that perverts truth shall soon be incapable of knowing the true from false. If you persist in wearing glasses that distort, everything will be distorted to you."

C. H. Spurgeon

---

205   John 18:38 (NASB)

YOUR TRUTH, MY TRUTH

Are there single, particular, individual truths that define and govern reality or is truth, as Hobbes puts it, "general, eternal and immutable?"[206] Questions concerning truth, such as—Does truth exist? Is truth objective or subjective? What is truth? and Can truth be known?—have been contemplated and argued since early man walked the earth. The nature, substance, and existence of truth is something that we all ponder at some point in our life.

I argue that truth is only possible in the understanding of God. God is the bedrock of truth, both in His being and in our reality. Outside of this foundation, truth will begin to disintegrate. It is not because it fails to be, but rather man fails in his ability to find it.

When man has no anchor by which to hold an idea as profound as reality, confusion sets in and the mind becomes unhinged and fractured. There is nothing by which to grasp a hold of, and therefore, the foundation is subject to wild questions, such as "How do I know that I am here?" or "How do I know that I exist?" How can you reason the idea of reality without the self to reason? Questions like these are a natural byproduct of confusion from loss of a God perspective. Clearly, how can man know anything for certain if there is no foundation by which it is fixed.

We can argue that truth is proven through sense and experience, logical standards, agreement with observable facts, an accord with the mind, etc., but without an anchor, truth hangs in the air, like a picture

---

206   Adler, p. 918

without a frame, held without a wall. Man no longer recognizes that the divine gifts of reason, agreement, logic, and wisdom allow us to distinguish absolute truth from error, feeling, or opinion. Our mind then is left without a firm foundation, like a house built on sand.

Thomas Aquinas said, "Divine truth has no source. It is not truth by correspondence with anything else. Rather it is, in the language of the theologian, the "primal truth." God Himself, who is the primal truth…is the rule of all truth, and the principle and source of all truth."[207] In God, truth is found to be existent, knowable, immutable, and eternal. It then has the ability to answer all the questions about reality that we contemplate.

I AM THE TRUTH:

In John 14:6, Jesus makes an extraordinary personal claim. *"Jesus said to him I am the way, and the truth, and the life; no one comes to the Father but through Me."*[208] This claim is unique in that He states that salvation is exclusively in Him, that He is literally absolute reality—truth itself, that He is the genesis of life—life itself, and that only by Him, man comes to the Father. While we see these claims throughout the New Testament, in this one verse, Jesus exclaims His power and relevance so that man can understand His significance.

Furthermore, Jesus' claim of truth is not about His knowledge of truth but specifically His substance. Jesus is saying that He *is* all truth and that He *is* all reality. This is the point Aquinas was making. Truth is not a thing, it is a He.

207   Adler, p. 918
208   John 14:6 (NASB)

We read throughout the New Testament of Jesus being truth, speaking truth, or truth coming through Jesus:

1. Noted by others as a speaker of the truth - Once in Matthew, twice in Mark

2. Noted by others as truly, the son of God - Twice in Matthew, once in Mark

3. Said to teach the way of God in truth - Once in Luke

4. Noted by others as truly the prophet - Twice in John

5. Noted by others as being full of grace and truth - Once in John

6. Spoke truth with authority - "Truly I said to you" - 27 total times between Gospels (14 x Matthew, 7 x Mark (5 unique), 6 x Luke (5 unique))

7. Spoke truth with authority - "Truly, truly I said to you" - 21 times in John (19 unique)

8. Jesus claimed He spoke truth - Four times in John

9. Jesus said His testimony is true - Once in John

10. Jesus claimed to *be* truth - Once in John

11. Jesus claimed to bear witness to the truth - Once in John

Said of Jesus:

1. Full of truth - Once in John

2. Truth came through Jesus - Once in John

3. Truth is in Jesus - Once in Ephesians

The ancient Greece philosopher Gorgias wrote: "*Nothing Exists. Even if something exists, nothing can be known about it. Even if something can be known about it, knowledge about it can't be communicated to others. Even if it can be communicated, it cannot be understood.*" There are many problems with his line of reasoning but the clearest problem exists in his original argument "Nothing exists." Nothing, by nature, can not exist. If it exists, it is no longer nothing, but something. If something exists, it can be found. If it can be found, it can be known. This is the same understanding with truth.

Truth exists, because God exists. Its reality rests in the existence of God. In this way, there is no "my truth, your truth." There is only, "The Truth." It exists whether we accept it or not, because it is not bound by the limitations of our reasoning or will. It is eternal and transcendent, because it is of God.

Because truth has a foundation, it is knowable and obtainable. I can know absolutely that I exist; I can know absolutely that you exist, and I can know absolutely that life exists. I know (aware) because I know (exist). I reason, recognize, and resolve, because I have an anchor that grounds my thinking. It allows me to dig deeper into the harder questions. I can uncover more and ask more, because there exists a place of finding. This allows me to come to a place of conclusion, move forward, and build upon. How can you ever build on a bottomless nothing or furthermore solve and defend it? It is impossible. It is only with cornerstones of truth and reality that man can even begin to discover and explore. It is a fundamental bedrock that cannot exist apart from the truth giver—God.

TRUTH - EVIDENCE OF GOD

Truth is evidence of God. Its existence assumes God's existence. If there was no truth, man would not be able to consider truth's possibility. We reason about truth only, because there is something to reason about. The absolute nature of truth exists, because it was given by Someone greater who possessed the substance, knowledge, wisdom, and capacity to give it. By necessity, truth is of God, because it is the only way that reality can be anchored. By reason of observation, we know reality is anchored. It is self-answering.

If God did not exist, there would be no foundation, anywhere, in any place, at any time, by which to measure or know truth. However, we know truth is measurable and knowable. For example, we know there are truths in science, math, logic, and morality. We know it is true that you are reading this book right now. That is an example of a measurable, observable truth. Truth exists, and our reality supports this assertion.

PERSONAL VERSUS UNIVERSAL

Two important facts concerning the nature of truth is its immutability and that it is not subject to man's knowledge, will, or acceptance for its confirmation. This is a foundational deviation from man's false thinking that truth is determined by personal measures and standards. In our culture that regards man's reasoning above all else, truth can be trusted, even if it is not popular. It is not shifting and foolish. You can be sure of its footing, even when everyone is going the other way. I can know that abortion is wrong, even if the culture says it's right. Its truth lies in the biblical understanding that it is something God hates: "*There are six things that **the Lord hates**, seven that are an abomination to him: haughty eyes, a lying tongue, and **hands that shed innocent blood**.*"[209] The truth of its immorality is factual not emotional. As a result, we can stand in the gap, against the tide, despite every push back that comes our way.

While there are personal truths, i.e., it is true that I love chocolate, this is different than global/universal "Truth." Personal truths are not bound by an eternal standard; nor do the ramifications and consequences have the same effect when you do not believe them or if you violate them. For example, it is true that I love chocolate, but it *is* ok if you do not. However, if you believe pedophilia is okay, then it is irrelevant how you feel because pedophilia is wrong. Your truth is not "Truth", it is error. I do not care how strongly you believe it or how much you feel it is right.

Personal truths are limited, changing, and temporary. They are qualified by and dependent on you. Eternal truths are qualified by their Maker. Their maker must be equivalent in being to establish them. There is only One eternal being with that quality, and that is God.

NO GREATER QUESTION ASKED

In John 18:38, we read:

"Therefore Pilate said to Him, 'So You are a king?'

Jesus answered, 'You say correctly that I am a king. For this I have

---

209   Proverbs 6:16-17 (ESV)

been born, and for this I have come into the world, to testify to the truth. Everyone who is of the truth hears My voice.'

Pilate said to Him, 'What is Truth?'"[210]

What a powerful question Pilate asked Jesus; however, he walked away before hearing Jesus Christ's response: "I AM...THE TRUTH."[211] Jesus was born to testify about Himself.

Jesus is the anchor by which we know reality. His time on the earth clarified, personified, and demonstrated truth. He holds the characteristics by which truth is known and in which its standards are held. He is eternal, immutable, knowable, not subject to man—you can sense and experience Him. He does not contradict logical standards. His life agrees with observable facts, and His truth is in accord with the mind.

Scottish preacher John Duncan said, "Christ either deceived mankind by conscious fraud, or He was Himself deluded and self-deceived, or He was Divine. There is no getting out of this trilemma. It is inexorable."[212] It is similar to C.S. Lewis's famous statement that Jesus is a Liar, lunatic, or Lord. In reference to His claim of truth, Jesus cannot be truth and not be truth. And He can't be moral and good and be a spreader of dishonest claims. Additionally, Jesus being considered exclusively as a moral teacher is never how Jesus was viewed. As C.S. Lewis noted, "We may note in passing that He was never regarded as a mere moral teacher. He did not produce that effect on any of the people who actually met him. He produced mainly three effects—

---

210   John 18:38 (NASB)

211   John 14:6 (NASB)

212   Duncan, John. *Colloquia Peripatetica*, Edinburgh: Edmonston and Douglas, 1870. p. 109

Hatred—Terror—Adoration. There was no trace of people expressing mild approval."[213]

People argue the logic behind this trilemma, but you are left to recognize an error in thinking if you accept one aspect of Jesus but reject the other. Either side you choose recognizes one of two possibilities: faith in Jesus has either led more people astray to eternal damnation than any cult leader before or after Him, or He is indeed exactly who He claimed to be—"the Way, the Truth, and the Life." He is either Truth, or He is man's greatest deceiver but He cannot be both. Which leaves man to answer how a great deceiver could have a global and universal impact for good. Jesus changed the way we view life, humanity, love, peace, kindness, sacrifice, forgiveness and value. How could He heal the broken and the love the loveless unless He is everything He claimed to be? As we are told in Matthew 7:18 "A good tree cannot bear bad fruit, nor *can* a bad tree bear good fruit."[214]

No man has ever been able to cast a valid claim of sin or falsehood against Jesus. Like Pilate, history stands saying "I find no guilt in this man."[215] He alone claimed to be truth, and also embodied and fulfilled its requirements.

*"So Jesus was saying to those Jews who had believed Him, "If you continue in My word, then you are truly disciples of Mine; **and you will know the truth, and the truth will make you free**.'"*[216]

---

213   http://www.christasus.com/letters/cslwhatarewetomakeofjesuschrist.htm Accessed October 2018

214   Matthew 7:18 (NKJV)

215   Luke 23:4 (ESV)

216   John 8:31-32 (NASB)

THE GOD WE NEED

"One can't prove that God doesn't exist, but science makes God unnecessary."[217]

Steven Hawkings

---

217 https://abcnews.go.com/GMA/stephen-hawking-science-makes-god-unnecessary/story?id=11571150, Accessed 1 October 2019

I have heard people argue that the theory of evolution makes God unnecessary. They say that within the scope of evolutionary science lies the deathblow of the need for God, and therefore, God does not exist. Let's consider the strength of this argument. First, let me point out that this idea of evolutionary science removing the need for God is an opinion, not a fact. Even if evolutionary science was completely uncontested, it couldn't negate the reality of God because the evolution argument lies squarely in "how" we and this universe came to be. The reality and question of God's existence lies beyond that argument. It does not rest in function but in being. This is often confused.

Second, there is no measure by which science can emphatically say that God does not exist, as it does not have the knowledge or ability to do so. As a result, any statement about God's nonexistence is purely conjecture. Even if evolutionary science proved that we don't need God to be here, we are still left with the fact that need and have are not equal.

Lastly, because we are limited in knowledge, we are unaware of the full scope of our need to be able to say with certainty that we do not need God. Our knowledge is limited to what we have the means to discover. We are observing a universe abounding with information beyond our present understanding and capabilities and we are foolish to assume that those limitations don't restrict us. As Thomas Edison noted, "We don't know a millionth of one percent about anything."[218] As a result of our limitations, any statement about our lack of apparent need for God is also conjecture.

---

218   *Golden Book,* Apr. 1931

NEED VS HAVE

There are many creatures in existence that are unaware of information and facts in their present reality. Take hydrothermal microorganisms as an example. These creatures "...do not need light, and they do not need oxygen, and the Earth's interior provides them with heat, so they can live without the sun."[219] While these microorganisms don't directly need light energy, it still exists within their present reality. The sun exists and is present whether these microorganisms know it or directly need it.

Additionally, no matter how indirect their need of the sun, their existence and purpose rests on the fact that they do indeed "have" it. Without the presence of the sun in our solar system, no life could exist on this earth. Their indirect need has no bearing on the fact that the sun's light energy warms the globe so that life can inhabit the earth. The reality of the sun is not subject to the awareness of their needs. In short, they need the sun even if they don't know they do.

This is true of us as well. We only discover what is already present and existing in the universe, yet our need occurs before and in spite of our knowledge. It is not our detection that ushers forces like gravity into reality anymore than our lack of awareness negates them. The fact is they exist apart from our known need or understanding. Concerning reality, Ethan Siegel writes, "Reality is a complicated place. All we have to guide us, from an empirical point of view, are the quantities we can measure and observe. Even at that, those quantities are only as good

219   http://scienceline.ucsb.edu/getkey.php?key=5412 Accessed 27 August 2019

as the tools and equipment we use to make those observations and measurements...We also can't observe or measure everything. Even if the Universe weren't subject to the fundamental quantum rules that govern it, along with all its inherent uncertainty, it wouldn't be possible to measure every state of every particle under every condition all the time. At some point, we have to extrapolate. This is incredibly powerful and incredibly useful, but it's also incredibly limiting."[220]

All our lack of awareness does is limit our knowledge and expose the ignorance of our need, it has no bearing on the existence of what is undiscovered. This is how reality is absolute. To put it another way, Schrödinger's cat is either dead or alive concretely, our knowledge has no bearing on that nor can change that truth.

In the same way, we can't say that we don't have God merely because evolutionary science believes it has proven that we don't need Him. To be certain, the idea that we don't need God is a position of belief, anchored by faith and not fact. It stems from purely scientific parameters by people who have chosen to reject the numerous evidence that proves God's existence. Since science is meant to measure the natural not the supernatural, it is incapable of truly considering the question of God. As the National Academy of Sciences and Institute of Medicine noted, "Science can neither prove nor disprove religion.... many religious beliefs involve entities or ideas that currently are not within the domain of science. Thus, it would be false to assume that all

---

220   https://www.forbes.com/sites/startswithabang/2017/11/22/scientific-proof-is-a-myth/#6e-471aba2fb1 Accessed 11 August 2019

religious beliefs can be challenged by scientific findings."[221] However, its inability to measure the supernatural has no bearing on the reality of it.

Like the hydrothermal microorganisms mentioned before, our need is real in spite of our lack of awareness. This is the beauty of reality. Its purpose is to act as an anchor and a true compass. A.W. Tozer wrote on the nature of reality, "What do I mean by reality? I mean that which has existence apart from any idea mind may have of it, and which would exist if there were no mind anywhere to entertain a thought of it. That which is real has being in itself. It does not depend on the observer for its validity."[222] This is the point behind God's declared word of Himself when He said to Moses, "I am that I am."[223] God alone is self-existent and does not need for us to believe Him for it to be true. However, we are not the same. We may be wholly unaware of our need for God, but God's being demands that our need is true. Since He alone is self existent, we could not be without Him. His very existence demands our need for Him.

OUR VERY REAL NEED

We are told throughout Scripture that God is the creator of four powerful components of our universe—matter, space, time and energy. As this is so, God is therefore needed for the very existence of all that is, whether or not we believe it to be true. Assuming that scientists could theorize a way for these components to be without God, is not

221 http://www.nas.edu/evolution/FAQ.html Accessed 11 August 2019
222 The Pursuit of God, A.W. Tozer
223 Exodus 3:14 (KJV)

the same as saying that they *are* without God. These are not equal statements. Nothing can prove that God didn't intend for it to be that way. I can easily argue that God set in motion a universe capable of coming into existence exactly the way that it did and that there is no science to disprove that thought. The probabilities can be argued back and forth but we are left with a truth—the probability exists. This is why even Richard Dawkins admits that he can't say for certain God doesn't exist[224],

The actuality of God can't be eliminated even when we consider the most interesting scientific arguments of the universe's origins. Consider String Theory as an example. "Hugh Everett III proposes that the wavefunction never actually collapses, but all possibilities become actualities— just in alternate realities. The universe is continually splitting apart as every quantum question is resolved, in every possible way across an immense Multiverse of parallel universes."[225] Based on this theory, there are parallel universes where *every possibility becomes an actuality*. Therefore, the actuality of God exists in a parallel universe. With that reality exists not just any God, but the God who created matter, space, time and energy. Furthermore, this theory would mean that the God who is above all, infinite, eternal, almighty, all powerful, omniscient, omnipresent, does exist. It would logically follow that by His very nature, He would still be God over all realities and possibilities in any multiverse. Therefore, He would still be God in this universe

---

224   https://www.telegraph.co.uk/news/religion/9102740/Richard-Dawkins-I-cant-be-sure-God-does-not-exist.html Accessed September 30, 2019

225   https://www.dummies.com/education/science/physics/string-theory-the-many-worlds-interpretation/ Accessed 8 August 2019

even if He exists in a parallel one.

As you can see, whether God exists in a parallel universe or realm is irrelevant. In the same way, whether we think we need God is inconsequential, because our very existence is created and upheld by God Himself. Furthermore, due to His function as Creator and Sustainer, we do need Him to exist, regardless if we are unaware of that fact. While it is true that God has required faith to come to Him, His certainty is removed from it. Faith is not the force that creates God rather it is the gift that allows us to believe in Him. God is, by nature and being, certain!

There will never be a scientific way to measure or a theory to disprove what is infinitely powerful and uncontainable. No test will ever invade the holy realm of God to take a measurement of His being. You can't measure the infinite any more than you can capture what is spirit. His truth has been revealed in His Word and the testimony of His people have proven it. His presence is available to anyone with a humble and seeking heart. Knowing God is not and will never be scientific, it is a measure of faith, rooted deep in the soul and spirit of a man. The amazing grace is that this overwhelmingly powerful and uncontainable God, beckons man to come.

"God has objective existence independent of and apart from any notions which we have concerning Him. The worshipping heart does not create its Object."[226]

A.W. Tozer

---

226   The Pursuit of God, A.W. Tozer

Made in the USA
Middletown, DE
18 December 2021

56455360R00126